Reflections on My Way Home

To Joyce,

Gods' Blessings!

Jay Fansler

Book by the same author:

On My Way Home

REFLECTIONS

ON MY WAY HOME

REV. JAY SAMONIE

ISBN 0-7392-0486-6
Library of Congress Catalog Card Number: 99-97067

Printed in the United States of America by

MORRIS PUBLISHING
3212 East Highway 30
Kearney, Nebraska 68847
800-650-7888

ACKNOWLEDGMENTS

There are many brother priests who have expressed their moral support to my first book *On my Way Home* and encouraged me to keep writing. I am especially grateful to Bishop Joe Schoenherr and Msgr. Ken Michael as well as my priestly colleagues: Reverends David Brock, James Curtin, James Cusack, Joseph Ferens, Al Gitzen, Randall Joyce, Ray Moeggenberg, Daniel Murphy, Richard Rakoczy, and Joseph Schabel. Sisters Monica Kostielney, Kathy Peatee, and Carol Campbell were equally positive and encouraging as were Anne Wozny, Pat La Fontaine and Jude Ripley.

My gratitude extends to Karyn Nader, Jack and Ronnie Morgan, Maxine Paus and Bea Marx for editing and proofreading the manuscript, and Sally Owen, for helping to organize my material for this second book.

THIS BOOK IS DEDICATED TO:

the Lord Who has gifted me
with guidance and miraculous experiences
from early childhood,

His Angelic and Saintly Helpers,

and to all those who,
having read my first book,
encouraged me to keep writing.

CONTENTS

AUTHOR'S NOTE

There was a common theme in the responses of those who read my first book *On My Way Home*. Many of those who gave me feedback, either by word or in writing, were saying in so many words: *You have helped me to believe that God is never far away! But what about me? How do I get closer to God? How do I become aware of His Presence? Am I fulfilling the purpose for which I was born? How do I discover my next step on my way Home? Can you teach us to meditate?* And many more such questions. These are some of the questions that motivated me to write another book. It was truly initiated by my readers.

There is a deep hunger prevalent in humanity to receive some kind of affirmation from God. Sometimes, people believing they are ready for spiritual contact, place themselves in awkward situations. I was told that after reading my first book, one lady stayed up practically all night, waiting for a possible visit from someone in the spirit world, or maybe having an overpowering sense of Divine Presence. She was waiting for the slim but exciting possibility of witnessing something mystical. Unfortunately, nothing happened. Sad to say, we can't make such things happen! I, for one, know that very well! And, as for waiting for something extraordinary to happen, I am sorry to say that one may have to wait a very long time, since God's time and ours are not the same at all. In fact, what we are expecting may not happen in the near future and there is no certainty that it will ever happen—or, on the other hand, mystical experiences can happen right this moment! We never know...

In my first book, On My Way Home, I repeated what two great teachers shared with us at the University of Detroit on the topic of Mysticism: *The most we can do, is to set up the conditions for the possibility of having a mystical experience.* We simply cannot control the outcome!

If we could *make* the experience happen, it would have to be classified as an experience with the *ego* as the source. Our own conscious mind or ego is capable of making up what would appear to be a spiritual or mystical event if one desired strongly enough. Our ego has the ability to give birth to an experience, cause it and execute it. But, in such a case, nothing really occurs which contributes to our spiritual growth. As a matter of fact, we would *regress* by *forcing* our will or our imagination to produce such an activity—the result being an act of *arrogance* rather than *Divine Guidance.*

Only when we allow God, or one of His Saintly Helpers to

be the source of a truly *surprising* and spiritual experience far beyond our expectations, does the experience become *real, productive, redemptive— and touching the very depths of our souls. Patience* is the key word here! There are no short-cuts, bargains or special deals! It would be like demanding that a flower bloom before its time!

As a matter of fact, I have wondered many times: *Why have these extraordinary experiences been happening to me? What is their purpose? Were they not beautiful gifts from the Heart of the Creator? And if they were gifts, why doesn't everyone receive them? Why me?* Every time I reflect on such questions, a most frightening thought occurs to me...the words of Jesus: "To whom much is given, much is expected." At times, I have to conclude: *Are these experiences a blessing or a burden?* With every gift comes an expected responsibility.

My greatest concern is whether or not I have lived a life consistent with what I believed and preached. Obviously, my life style is different from the average adult. Having never married, I am not in a position of having children and watching over them as they grow from infancy to adulthood nor having the comfort, security and warmth of a family gathered around me and my spouse as the years move on.

I do thank the Lord, however, that I was, at least, able to grow up in such an *atmosphere of love*, being the tenth child out of eleven. Three of my siblings died very early in life before

I was born. The eight of us grew up together with all the joys, sorrows, excitement, sadness and surprises that accompany life in a large family.

Being a priest, I also chose not to make a career in the world of business. My salary has been far below the level expected of a person with my educational background—one Doctorate and two Master Degrees—besides years of additional studies in Theology, Metaphysics, Scripture and Science on my own.

I am not mentioning the above to boast of a lifestyle that calls for God's *special blessing* or some *spiritual reward* for a good life! Quite the contrary! If living the life of a priest, with all its sacrifices and discipline, was so exceptional, so extraordinary, and so pleasing to God, then every priest, as a minister of God, should be blessed with spiritual and mystical experiences. But this is not so! Just being a priest does not earn rewards nor does it make a man holy, anymore than being the parent of a child, automatically makes the parent a responsible one. God does not simply reward a person for living out a chosen career, vocation or direction in life. This is what the Master said about God's servants in Luke 17:7-10:

> Who among you would say to your servant, who has just come in from plowing or tending sheep in the field, "Come here immediately and take your place at

table"? Would he not rather say to him, "Prepare something for me to eat. Put on your apron and wait on me while I eat and drink. You may eat and drink when I am finished!" Is he grateful to that servant because he did what was commanded? So should it be with you. When you have done all you have been commanded, say, "We are unprofitable servants; we have done what we were obliged to do."

The Jerome Commentary of the Bible adds to the above quote: "Addressed to the Apostles, this parable warns Church leaders, that they can never stop and rest in the belief that they have worked enough." I would extend this warning to anyone serving God.

I would therefore respond to anyone who happens to say to me: "God gave these miraculous experiences to you because you are a priest!" I cannot speak for all priests, but the ones I have known and questioned affirm that they had no such things happen to them. Yet, they would say that the Holy Spirit has been guiding and inspiring them all their lives but perhaps in a more subtle manner. Certainly, *everyone*— the married and the unmarried—are guided by the Holy Spirit. St. Paul says in Romans, 8:15:

For the Spirit that God has given you, does not

make you slaves and cause you to be afraid; instead, the Spirit makes you God's children, and by the Spirit's power we cry out to God 'Abba, Father!' God's Spirit joins Himself to our spirit to declare that we are God's children.

The Holy Spirit is the Universal Guide for all of us to recognize God as our Father. If God *rewards* people because of their faithfulness to their work or lifestyle, there are many persons I can think of that *deserve* much more than I have ever received. I am thinking of a person like Archbishop Romero, assassinated for his stand against injustice and crime; or a missionary, who is serving a horrible sentence in prison simply for preaching Christ in a foreign land; or a woman raising four or five children with no husband and pouring out her whole life in loving service to her children; or a person slowly losing the life force through a cancerous condition that diminishes life a little more each day. There are countless examples of heroic people offering their lives in loving and dedicated service.

My belief is that we do not earn gifts from God. They are just that...*gifts*. All the incredible situations and turning points in my life, in which God interrupted the normal course of events, would have to be called gifts. What else would you call a totally surprising and unexpected blessing? I thank the Lord every day for the wonderful ways in which His Divine

Providence touched my life. *Gratitude* is my principal prayer.

I still continue to search out the meaning of all that has happened to me. As far back as my memory can take me, all my life, even as a young child, I became aware that God was making Himself known to me through some extraordinary action. Yet, in my deepest soul-searching moments, I still experience some reluctance to believe that these incredible occurrences could actually happen to me. *But they did! And I will never deny it!*

On the other hand, something beautiful *did* take place. In spite of my personal doubts and concerns, I do have a clearer understanding of God's action in the world. Even when I feel nothing, I know that He is there! In fact, I feel sufficiently confident to branch out and study other ways of approaching God, to walk without fear into the unknown, to see that Eternal Truth is known by many different names among the cultures of the world. What was given to me was not just for me. No gifts are! Like the servant in the parable above, I am simply doing what is required of me. It makes me no better than you. We all have work to do, assigned by the Master.

It should be not be surprising, then, that I find no difficulty in remaining loyal to my Catholic beliefs and at the same time comfortably pursuing studies concerning metaphysical concepts; such as auras, chakras, psychic diagnosis, the possibility of past life and near-death experiences, A Course in Miracles (ACIM), the Silva Method of Mind Development, the Edgar Cayce Readings, mysticism, meditation, dreams and other topics, some of which I would like to address in this book. Each of the above offers a capsule of knowledge which makes me pause for reflection.

Rev. Jay Samonie
Westland, Michigan
August 15, 1999

PART ONE

One of my most important lessons in life was discovering that the world I knew was not fixed and complete. Beginning with the vision that I witnessed as a young boy along with my two sisters, Rose and Elizabeth, and my brother Tony, I had to make some radical changes in my view of what was real or unreal. After that experience, I had no doubt that there truly was a world of spirit going on right now and it was incredibly more beautiful and exciting than this one.

In Part One, I wish to share the amazing changes that took place within me as I realized more and more clearly from my experiences that I had to let go of many of my misconceptions concerning life and Reality.

For me, it was practically a lifetime before I became fully convinced that there was truly something *Out There*, that exists beyond the five senses. Being accustomed to believing only in what I can see, feel or touch, I had to take a giant leap of faith to give assent to realities that were far beyond the limits of my imagination.

I have always questioned the topics of a pre-planned destiny, receiving glimpses of the future, the concept of guilt, the need for change and the whole issue of death. These reflections seemed to be most urgent in my mind and so I am sharing them in these first chapters.

1. IS OUR FUTURE ALREADY WRITTEN?

All I have seen,
teaches me
to trust the Creator
for all I have not seen.

—Ralph Waldo Emerson

Much of what I wish to share through writing comes from actual experiences. The Seminary gave me a wonderful preparation for life as a clergyman, but little did we know about the surprises that awaited us as life made its turns in the labyrinth of time.

My oldest sister Marie passed away in October of 1980. That was one of the saddest days of my life. While I was at the funeral luncheon for my sister, there was a call from Holy Trinity Parish. They said it was very important.

"I have some bad news! Are you sitting down?" began Steve Esposito, who was answering the phone that day.

"What could be worse than what I am experiencing right now—at my sister's funeral?"

"It may not be worse. But it's bad. Sharon Szente just

died!"

I quickly interrupted: "You mean her mother. She had not been that well lately."

"No! It was the *daughter*, I'm sure! She was killed on the freeway going to your sister's funeral service."

My mind was reeling with thoughts. Sharon came to my sister's wake service the night before. She said she would attend the funeral the next morning, as she knew the family. *If, indeed, she did die, it would explain her absence at the funeral.*

I asked if he knew any of the details concerning her death. He said, "A truck, coming down the freeway from Zilwaukee, Michigan, lost one of its tires. The 150 pound tire hit the median on Interstate 75 and bounced about forty feet in the air, crashing directly into the windshield in front of Sharon at the wheel. She died instantly. She never knew what hit her." The next morning newspapers verified everything he had said.

But that is not the whole story! At the wake service, the night before, Sharon was telling us about the *appearances* of her father. Three weeks prior to that tragic event, Sharon said she was visited by her father in the middle of the night. (He had died about ten years before.) She was awakened by his presence. Naturally, although she loved her father and missed him a lot, she was genuinely shocked to see him.

"Am I going to die, dad? Is that why you are here?" she inquired, hesitating as she spoke.

"Not yet, my dear. But you will be joining us soon." She said he was surrounded by beautiful scenery with lively colors...emanating peace and security.

"Well, things are not going very well right now. Maybe it *is* time to leave this world. Can I think about it?" She waited for a response. He nodded in the affirmative and disappeared.

A week later, he appeared again, waking her up, as before. "Are you ready to join us now?" He asked.

She said that everything had improved in the past week. She got a job, she and her husband were doing very well and the kids were behaving better than ever. She expected him to say that she would not be leaving this world soon. He said her request would be considered and that he would get back to her. With that, he vanished.

Three days later, he appeared for the third time at the same hour. This time there was not much discussion. She was expecting an extension of time. That was not the message! Rather, he told her that *there was no more time!* She was destined to join him in the spirit world. And it would be soon.

"How soon?" She asked, as her whole body began shaking with fear. Even as she spoke to us, her voice was now quivering.

"Very soon! I cannot tell you the circumstances but it will be very *quick* and *unexpected.*

Looking back, that was exactly three days before her death.

She related to us how she began to wash the kitchen floor, wash the walls, vacuum, wash clothes and wrote notes to her husband where to find things in her absence. In other words, she was preparing to go on a one-way trip, right off the face of the earth!

On her way to my sister Marie's funeral service, she stopped to see a very close friend (and cousin, I believe) whose name was Connie. She spoke briefly: "There is something I want to share with you...I think I...never mind!" She never completed her sentence and left. It is the belief of those of us who knew her that she had the premonition that she had *a rendezvous with death*...that very day, that very hour! The only question was *how* it was going to happen.

This was an awful period of time for me. I was still grieving over the death of my sister Marie and there I am at another wake and funeral service a few days later. At Sharon's funeral, I mentioned the above story about the nightly visits from her father and it lessened the pain somewhat, knowing that her death was already predicted before it happened. It was not just an accidental death, in which the family would be raising their fists to the heavens, crying and shouting: "Why?" and "Where were you, God, when this terrible accident happened?"

Sharon's *destiny* on the highway was totally unpredictable, unnatural and unthinkable by human standards. Yet, it was foretold...and expected! She *prepared* for it without knowing the conditions or the details surrounding her departure into the spirit world.

When both funerals were history and I had a chance to think about what took place, I thought to myself: "If *just one person* can receive information about an impending death before it happens, then it must be true for others. Perhaps a larger percentage than we would expect! At some dimension of reality, our death is *already known*! Somewhere! Somehow! I wondered how many people have received direct knowledge of their death without sharing it with anyone, taking it to their graves with them. I am certain it did not only happen *once* in the history of the human race!

As a matter of fact, President John Kennedy was told by several psychics not to go to Dallas on that fatal day. He heard them; he knew what the dreadful result could be if he did not listen: "If you must go, then use the bullet-proof bubble!" He ignored such warnings and met his fate that day. But that tragic event was foreseen and reported in advance. Just how much is known about our future here on earth? I have asked myself that question many times.

Whenever I am confronted with unusual events, such as the above, it makes me pause in silence for a moment and re-think my convictions. I end up as usual...with more questions than answers—enough questions to warrant the writing of this book. I have always believed in the Communion of Saints. In fact, that is part of the Creed. Practically every religion believes that we survive death. If this is so, then why would we be unable to communicate with each other. Spirits may not have a *physical body*, but they certainly do have a *mind*. Mind to mind perception or ESP is accepted in most circles as a fact. The Bible is full of such conversations, such as Moses and God, Jesus and Elijah, Mary and the Angel Gabriel.

I have been wondering...whether spirits, living outside of time in the spirit world, would be able to know the past, present and future in a single glance. If they do, they can become awesome guides for us. Our loved ones who have passed on, may not be permitted to reveal our future, in detail, to us, but they could, at least, guide us in the right direction.

2. LETTING GO OF THE PAST

The Body of B. Franklin, Printer
(Like the cover of an old book,
its contents torn out,
and stript of its lettering and gilding)
lies here, food for worms.
But the Work shall not be lost;
for it will, (as he believed),
appear once more
in a new and elegant Edition,
revised and corrected, by the Author.
　　　　—Benjamin Franklin's own epitaph

"Let the dead bury the dead." This is another way of saying—freely paraphrased—*"Let go of the past."* We often hear those redundant words:

"This is the way we used to do it!"
"I have always believed that since I was a child."
"I grew up in that culture."

Let the dead bury the dead is a clear challenge—almost a defiance—of breaking with the cultural and traditional beliefs we all grow up with, especially in a family with strong ethnic ties. In today's world, the challenge emerges frequently as we witness our own American culture going through rapid changes in values and direction.

We have learned to live side by side with various cultures and subcultures all around us. People living next door, or a few houses away, often exhibit an entirely different style of life, speak a foreign tongue and most likely, follow a religion not of our persuasion.

In my early childhood, I knew a different world. Eggs were only forty-four cents per dozen, bread was eight cents and a U.S. stamp was two cents. There were no jet planes or television; space ships (except in *Flash Gordon* adventures) and computers were unheard of. We did not own a car! The classiest form of communication was the radio and thank God for the movie theaters. I am talking about the days of Bette Davis, Clark Gable, Humphrey Bogart and a host of other actors who remain to this day, second to none.

It is no wonder that we all lived in our nice little homes, knowing very little about our neighbors and the rest of the world, just as in the movie *Pleasantville*. I learned to *let go* as a youngster. I saw conflict with some of the values and culture of my parents—thoroughly Lebanese in nature—with the *American way of life*. My father generally spoke Arabic to me, and I understood him. I never spoke back in Arabic, and I still cannot speak it today. I was born in America, enjoyed American music and had to make some important adjustments concerning culture and belief.

To become disciples of Jesus, some of His followers had to face this same dilemma. Here is the text in which these words are found (Luke 9:57-62) :

As they were proceeding on their journey, someone said to Him, "I will follow you wherever you go." Jesus answered him, "Foxes have dens and birds of the sky have nests, but the Son of Man has nowhere to rest His head." And to another He said, "Follow Me." But he replied, "Lord let me go first and bury my father." But He answered him, "Let the dead bury their dead. But you, go and proclaim the kingdom of God."

Jesus was presenting a great challenge to his audience. Among the Jewish people of His time, there was a very strong tie to family and relatives. It was expected of every young man to be responsible for the burial of his father. Culturally, it was unthinkable to just leave the family and follow an itinerant teacher. Jesus defied a centuries-old custom.

According to the Jerome Commentary, He was saying in clearer language: *Let the spiritually dead bury the physically dead.* Jesus had the words of life and He invited his listeners to go forth and proclaim the Kingdom of God. It was a play on words, not to be taken literally, but to get those present thinking about the importance of spreading words of hope to others.

I had always struggled with that phrase. I came from a Middle East family with strong ties to my parents, siblings and relatives. It was a monumental decision to leave home at the age of fifteen and board at the Seminary. I was home only for Christmas, Easter and summer vacation. For a young man that was quite a heavy cross to bear. It was always a struggle to continue living away from home, but I felt called to the priesthood.

Fr. Randall Joyce often spoke of Jesus as the greatest *possibility-thinker* that ever lived. That is so very true! There were no limits to His thinking. Jesus not only believed that *"All things are possible with God,"* but that His whole life was a testimony of that truth. Jesus consistently broke with long-standing and powerful traditions. He shocked His listeners often, and was in a sense, *excommunicated* from the Temple. He was "defiled" in more ways than one: talking privately to a Samaritan woman, curing the sick on the Sabbath, ignoring the ritual washings and speaking of God as His Father. In general, His whole *way of life* was a threat to his more conservative listeners!

Someone handed me a copy of the following recently:

"Next prisoner, come forward! You are charged," said the Grand Inquisitor, "with encouraging people to break the laws, traditions, and customs of our holy religion. How do you plead?"

"Guilty, your Honor."

"And with frequenting the company of heretics, prostitutes, public sinners, tax-collectors and the colonial conquerors of our nation—in short, the excommunicated. How do you plead?"

"Guilty your Honor."

"Also with publicly criticizing and denouncing those who have been placed in authority within the Church of God. How do you plead?"

"Guilty, your Honor."

"Finally, you are charged with revising, correcting, calling into question the sacred tenets of our faith. How do you plead?"

"Guilty, your Honor."

"What is your name, prisoner?"

"Jesus Christ, your Honor."

The above makes me pause! I have found it healthy to revisit my belief system every so often. I began to see more and more clearly that we are not living in a static Universe. There was so much more to see, if only we opened our eyes to the realities around us. People from all walks of life have a gift to present to us. I did believe, at one time for example, that the future could not be known. It was simply out of our reach; it was God's territory, and we were *out of bounds* if we tried to know something before it happened.

Life was saying something different to me. Still, it was not easy to break the mold of limited thinking. *I could not let go*, even as I kept meeting people who were gifted with *insight*. There was always someone who was ready to tell me, among other things, about my next assignment as a priest. I recall one evening, as I was on my way to bowl with the Hungarian League from Holy Cross, I stopped to have supper with an Italian friend Bella Gulli and her parents. They made the most delicious and authentic pasta. This took place in 1968, about a year or more before I had some mystical experiences. I was not ready for what took place. As I was finishing my meal, a friend of the family I was visiting happened to stop by. It was someone I had never seen before. It was perfectly clear that we had never met.

I will call her Helena to protect her real name. She was very short and wore a babushka that hid much of her face. She had beady eyes that seemed to stare at you, rather than look at you. She was dark-complected and appeared to be Italian, as well. The mother of the family living there asked me if I wanted a cup of tea. I replied in the affirmative. A lot of tea leaves were poured into my cup with the water. I was genuinely surprised!

I was expecting tea bags or, at least, the use of a strainer.

Bella was the one who invited me to the dinner. She proceeded to ask if I wanted Helena to give me a *tea reading*. I laughed a little and said quite clearly that I did not believe in that sort of thing. I said that was usually reserved for party games or a joke. The look on their faces did not give me that message. They were serious! I did not want to offend them, so I said, "Sure, if she wants to." I repeated, again, that I did not believe that people could read the future.

Helena had me turn the cup upside down and wait a few moments. Then I handed it to her after the tea had poured out and only the tea leaves remained inside the cup. She looked at it as if she were seeing things in the cup. I was on the other side of a rather long table and watched her closely, while holding back a burst of laughter that was ready to happen any moment. Remember, this woman did not know who I was or what kind of work I did. I was introduced as "Jay", and I had a bowling shirt on with the sponsor's name on the back.(I believe it was one of the Breweries.)

Then she spoke! She said: "I have never seen this sign before, in all the years I have been reading tea leaves..." I interrupted her and added "I am sure you tell this to everyone, right?" She affirmed that it was truly the first time she had seen a white lamb in a cup.

"Really?" I said doubtfully. I was sure she was making it

up. I hated to discredit what Helena said, but I could not resist the temptation to ask if I could take a look. She said: "Please do!"

I walked over to the other side of the table and looked at the area she pointed to. I could not believe my eyes! I looked again! There, in the cup, was a perfect picture of a lamb. It was outlined by the tea leaves and appeared to be white, since the cup was white. The face, the four legs, the shape...they were all perfect. There was no doubt whatsoever. It was a *white lamb!* I returned to my seat, completely confused. She got my attention! So I asked what did it mean? She said it was probably the luckiest sign anyone could ever have. She said "I think the Lamb of God is watching over you."

I was not very kind. I said, "I suppose one of the ladies told you who I am and what kind of work I do." She said "No!" And the three other adults in the house also insisted that she did not know who I was.

Helena spoke up again: "The second best sign you could have is the image of a horse in your cup. And that is what I am looking at."

I jumped in immediately: "Now, this has gone too far! I want to see the horse!" I got up and looked a second time. Sure enough, there was a perfect image of the face and neck of a horse. It was very clear.

Now I am not only confused. *I'm stunned!!! How could*

this be?, I asked myself. What was amazing about the whole thing, so far, was that she had not even begun the reading yet.

Then she began. "First of all, you are going to go south of the Border this summer. It will not be a long trip. Maybe a couple of weeks. Also, early next year, you will be given a promotion. I don't know what you do, but you will be pleased to have this higher position."

I interrupted her again! "I'm sorry, but I have absolutely no plans to go south of the Border this year and certainly not this summer! Also, there is no such promotion I could possibly be expecting. You must not be reading it right or else there is nothing there."

She held her ground. "Let's wait and see." With that, I left for the bowling alley.

The bowling season was over, finally, around the middle of May. In July, I was placed in charge of the Hispanic Apostolate for six months and moved to St. Bernadette's Church in Dearborn. I developed a team of co-workers. Of the seventeen team members about ten of us were asked—a total surprise!— to fly down to Mexico for a two-week intensive study of Scripture and how to establish *Comunidades de Base*— similar to Bible Study Groups—in the home. It was especially designed for Hispanics.

It was only after I was on the plane going south that I remembered the words that Helena had said. This was a genuine revelation to me! She was absolutely correct; she even gave the time of the year that I was going south. And Mexico was certainly south!

Several months later—in January of 1969— I was named Pastor of St. Bernadette Parish. It was indeed a promotion! As a matter of fact, I became, at that time, the youngest Pastor in the Archdiocese of Detroit. Because I was so young, I was told by my superiors that I would have to be called an *Administrator*, but I had all the rights and privileges of a Pastor.

She was right again!

There's more!!! The very first Sunday I was installed at St. Bernadette Parish as Pastor/Administrator, I was in procession down the aisle after Mass and was greeting the people as they were leaving church. Who did I see standing in line to be greeted by the new Pastor? *Yes, it was Helena. I would have recognized her anywhere!*

On the other hand, she apparently did not recognize me. There I was, wearing *priestly robes* instead of a *bowling shirt*!

She said, "Father, my name is..."

"Helena!" I chimed in.

"You know me?" She was puzzled. Obviously, she did not recognize me in this new setting. Sacred vestments and bowling shirts are not exactly look-a-likes!

"Yes, I know you, Helena. You gave a tea cup reading for me at Bella's house about eight or nine months ago, and ..."

Then it dawned on her who I was. She began mumbling, "Please forgive me! O Lord, I'm sorry, I'll never do that again. Please forgive me." She was repeating these words or words similar to them and making the sign of the cross continuously without stopping.

I said "Helena, God is not going to punish you. And there is nothing to forgive. You were absolutely right in everything you said to me." I told her about the trip to Mexico and then "being promoted" as she put it. I said "You have a gift from God. There are many fakes out there, but you were very accurate. You should use the gift God gave you. You did not ask for any money. You were simply using a gift that many people would love to have. They only dream about it."

"You think so, Father?" she said with such innocence. I had to reassure her again.

I found out later that Helena had a very hard life. She had been ridiculed because of her very small stature and had suffered a lot in her life. She was living in a very unhappy marriage and surviving in an abusive situation. In the midst of the darkness all around her, she was encouraged by an incredible ability to counsel people who came to her for help. She was honest and authentic in my opinion.

Speaking about people who tell me where my next move will be, without me even asking, I came across another person with an unusual psychic ability. Her name was Rose. She, too, had a hard life. She came to the United States from the Middle East, and she was raising three sons by herself when I first met her. Since we both traced our heritage to the Middle East, we became friends and remained friends until her death in 1997.

I was speaking to her one day while I was stationed at Holy Trinity in downtown Detroit. She made an off-hand remark: "You will be leaving Trinity soon and going to a church named after a warrior."

"There are no warrior Saints except...maybe, St. Joan of Arc," I replied.

"No! It's a male," she insisted. "He has a sword in his hand...wings on his back and he has one foot resting on the body of somebody real ugly."

There was no doubt in my mind. I quickly responded that she was describing St. Michael the Archangel. I asked if that is who she meant. She told me that she did not know who St. Michael was, and no name was given.

I added that she was probably talking about St. Michael Church in Pontiac—the parish I had just left when I came to Holy Trinity. I figured she was talking about the past, not the future. But she remained firm in her prediction that it was my next assignment...in the future.

One year later, I was reassigned. My superior sent me to Monroe, Michigan. The name of the church was *St. Michael the Archangel*. She was right and there had not been even the slightest thought of going there at the time. As a matter of fact, I was shocked when I was transferred. I had no such intention to leave. I was hoping to stay at Holy Trinity Church for at least a few more years, but my health began to deteriorate, making it very difficult to remain there. The stress in the inner city, after eleven years at Holy Trinity (making it twenty-five years altogether in the inner city of Detroit), had taken its toll on my heart and general health condition. I passed out twice without warning and also had a few scares with a heart condition and high blood pressure.

The bottom line was that Rose had correctly seen the name of my future assignment. She had been correct on a few other items she predicted.

Another friend, who is not Catholic, and, therefore, knew less than Rose about Saints, also saw me going to a church named after a Saint who was a warrior. This time, however, he was seen with wings. I knew immediately who such a Saint would be. Again, St. Michael Church was in my future!

Thinking metaphysically, and on the mental plane of thought, I was slowly beginning to realize that the future is already here, and therefore, already known. Finding the right persons who are gifted, is not easy. Many make claims that cannot be verified as accurate. Somehow, authentic people were being placed in my path.

3. CARRYING THE BAGGAGE OF GUILT

The past is yours, learn from it.
The present is yours, fulfill it.
—Walter Fauntroy

I have taught the Silva Method of Mind Development and Stress Control for fifteen years. During that time, I acquired a great deal of knowledge about human nature. I did not make a special project out of studying the nature of a human being, but after witnessing the same negative reactions of people to certain topics and the low self-image the students had of themselves, I began to take notice.

The majority of persons attending the classes in Mind Development came from a variety of ethnic backgrounds. That is not surprising, since Metropolitan Detroit is known as a melting-pot of nationalities. Most of them were brought up in a strict atmosphere with many rules and regulations established by their particular belief system. The majority may have been Catholic, but practically every religion was represented.

I am not, in any way, saying that there is something wrong with having rules and laws to live by. The *essence* of Law and

Order demands it. I am referring to the fact that each religion, by its very nature, is separated from other religions by having a *particular set of laws, beliefs and policies* by which to live. Otherwise, there would only be *one* religion. What became increasingly obvious to me after teaching the Silva Mind Development Course, a forty-hour Course which I taught sixty times, was the connection between a sense of guilt and a poor self-image.

I am not using the word *guilt* in the sense of committing a sin and feeling guilty about it. That is the traditional and limited meaning of the word. Rather, I am focusing on the word *guilt* with a much larger meaning. Webster's Dictionary offers this as one of the definitions of guilt: "Feelings of culpability, especially for imagined offenses or from a sense of inadequacy." This is the aspect of guilt I am referring to, along with a feeling of being unworthy, insignificant, unholy, rejected, alone, fragmented, beyond help, etc. In this wider meaning of guilt, it harbors such questions, as:

"What is wrong with me?"

"Why is everyone else doing so well and I am getting nowhere?"

"Why do these things always happen to me?" (...implying that I am the only person to whom bad things happen.)

"Why doesn't God ever hear my prayer?" (...while everyone else has their prayers answered!)

"Why can't I do anything right?"

All of the above are only a morsel of the many expressions of guilt in the broader, metaphysical sense. These thoughts of guilt—real or imagined—are bound to affect one's self image greatly. The results could vary in the mind of one who feels such guilt, as that of being the biggest sinner in the world, being ugly, because a couple of people said so, going straight to hell when death calls and destined to be a loser.

The following is a true incident that happened during one of my Silva Mind Development Lectures. There were about seventy-five adults taking a class with me in Pontiac, Michigan. We were talking about *self-image* in the class and how the mind can play tricks on a person whose mind is covered with a blanket of guilt—in the broader sense. A beautiful young lady, who looked about thirty-five years old, stood up and admitted in front of everyone that she considered herself ugly. We all looked at each other in amazement, since, without the slightest doubt, she was, by far, the prettiest woman in the class.

I asked her why she thought she was ugly. She said that her mother always told her that she was overweight and definitely not pretty. In spite of the image planted in her mind, by her own mother, she did eventually get married, only to receive the same kind of treatment from her husband. Her husband emphasized that she was both *ugly* and *fat*! When this gorgeous lady—lovely, slender and attractive to behold—was told frequently, by both mother and husband that she was fat and ugly, a very strange self-concept was confirmed within her.

The view of herself became so affected by such negative treatment, that it caused a terrible effect in her life. Every time she looked in the mirror, *she was unable to see herself.* Her face simply disappeared! She could only see her body up to her neck. *Her face simply did not show up as a reflection in the mirror!* She was terribly frightened; she thought she was going to be punished in public because no one would be able to see her face. She had such a pleasant, innocent-looking face. At first, the whole class, including myself, were disbelieving. She couldn't possibly be serious.

She was *very* serious! To stand up in front of other people and admit her ugliness and shameful self-image—coupled with a deep sense of guilt, believing she deserved it—was probably the hardest thing she ever did in her life. It was only possible, because she said she felt loved and accepted by the group. We had gone through a series of conditionings or meditations, if you will, on loving, forgiving and accepting oneself. We emphasized that the past was gone. We live in the present moment, where we can enjoy peace of mind. In such a welcoming and loving atmosphere, she opened herself up to us. After we proclaimed our total acceptance of her as a loving, beautiful, attractive and gifted human being—which we sincerely believed she was—she said she felt truly loved for the first time in her life. Tears were flowing freely as she now saw herself as a totally different person.

The next weekend when we met, she raised her hand, got up slowly, and burst out with enormous joy that she had seen her face once again in the mirror. It had been a long time! She said she really *was* pretty. That was no surprise to us, but when she told us that she felt good about herself and no longer felt inadequate, alone, separated, inferior and so on, we applauded her loudly.

The baggage of guilt weighs heavily. Have you honestly ever asked yourself such questions as "What's wrong with me?" Then you may be carrying the same kind of unnecessary guilt as my friend above. Our self-image is quite fragile. Another way of looking at guilt is when frustration, anger, disgust, or the feeling of being limp or floundering follow the inability to change things around us. I am referring to unacceptable circumstances in our life, such as: conflict at home, a disgusting situation at work or very limited freedom because of multiple responsibilities. Briefly, the feeling of being a loser or inadequate, results when we are unable to change the *world*, *others* or our *own fixed attitude* in a given situation.

Strangely enough, our sense of carrying an unnecessary baggage of guilt and a poor self-image can be corrected by understanding that there are only two basic emotions: *Love* and *Fear*. The opposite of love is not *hate*, as many people would say. Perhaps, their conclusions come from life itself, having experienced what may be called a *love/hate relationship*. Often, spouses, whose marriage bond is based on *need* rather than *unconditional love*, hate each other when their needs are not met and love one another when they are. This sense of love and hate can go on for years. Such a situation can only be resolved by changing one's viewpoint. *A new belief system is necessary: The Lord, Who gave us life, is the Creator of the Universe.* Since *God is Love,* as St. John tells us in his Gospel, our true heritage comes from Divine Love. It can never change! We are an extension of God's Love...and will always be.

Whatever is seen through the eyes of love is seen correctly. Unconditional love is a divine viewpoint! The moment fear enters the mind, it becomes distorted. Fear is generated by the thought of separation from God, from the world, from a spouse, a boss, a co-worker, a neighbor...and even from our True Self or Higher Self. Once the frightening face of fear emerges, we are actually blinded from the truth. Seeing everything from a separated and negative point of view, fear makes us afraid of ourselves, because what is not a part of us can become our enemy. It is *the enemy* that is the cause of all our troubles! It would be very easy to hate this enemy and even attack the enemy before we are attacked.

So, we attack, try to hurt, cause pain to that enemy of ours. The enemy may be ourselves or it may be another. (If I can't find another, the devil is always a good one to blame!) Now, I feel guilty for having attacked myself, resulting in illness or for attacking another through anger and even violence.

Translating the above into a real life experience in marriage, it would go something like this: a husband and wife are *very much in love.* They get along fine and every day is better than before. They really never argue; the wife keeps quiet in tense situations and lets her husband have the last word. *He is always right* when they have a difference of opinion or attitude.

One day she goes to a Seminar that teaches people how to speak up and be more assertive. The next time she and her husband get into discussion, she says what she means and he gets a little upset.

"What did you say?"

"You heard me; I believe I have a right to my opinion," she responds. He is completely thrown off guard.

"But you never talked like this before!"

"Maybe it's time I grew up!"

Now, begins the first battle they had since they were married. Since they now have the feeling of being separate, they can both strike out at each other, saying things they would never have said before. The fear of being attacked, the fear of losing the argument, the fear of looking *wimpy* has changed everything now.

From that time on, whenever they have a verbal exchange

out of fear and not out of love, certain other emotions will become evident. They will be yelling out of hatred and anger, emotions that were unthinkable before. The baggage of guilt is now part of the problem. Neither one of them likes hurting the other. Yet, the problem is not resolved. In fact, now, the one will blame the other for all the misery that has taken place. This situation will not resolve itself until the basic expressions of love and forgiveness dominate their differences. True love dispels fear. Fear is the absence of love, just as darkness is the absence of light.

One of them has to make the first move to change this situation into a *holy relationship.* It is done, as mentioned, through love, forgiveness and understanding. Forgiveness of oneself is the first step in removing any feeling of fear and guilt. Once she forgives herself, that is, to see the truth of who she is—namely, a child of God, created in His Divine image and, therefore, invulnerable—she will observe everything differently...herself, her husband, God and the so-called world out there. It is not *denial* in the sense that it *never* happened. Rather, it is a *statement* that she chooses love, and with God's help, to forgive herself and to forgive her husband. She prays to see her relationship with her husband from a different point of view. She will then talk to her husband as if nothing happened. God then turns their bond into a holy relationship. In a very real sense, *love is letting go of fear, anger, violent thoughts* and the *guilt* that follows. Fear and the other negative emotions are seen as unreal, because they are the absence of unconditional love. Being the absence of something, they are really nothing! They are now seen for what they are: just negative thoughts or false impressions.

The husband, in this scenario, may or may not correspond with her change in mind and viewpoint. If he does, they will have some happy days ahead. If not, he may continue in his negative attitude; they may even have to leave each other! At some point in his life, however, he will seriously consider changing his point of view.

Each one of us is loved one hundred percent by our Divine Parent. God is incapable of unreal emotions such as fear and hate. Because we have them, does not mean *God is like us.* On the contrary, we are striving *to be like God*, to raise ourselves from the imaginary prison of being trapped in the bondage of darkness and separation. I will take this up again in the chapter—*Your God Is Too Small.*

Considering guilt from the viewpoint of time is also important. *This broad sense of guilt* is never experienced in the present moment. It always occurs in the past, either way back in our childhood, in our teenage years or a few years ago. It may also have been experienced last week or just last night. It really doesn't matter—as long as it was in the past. While people are in the act of doing something, they believe that what they are doing is acceptable in the present moment, whether it is lying to get out of something, engaging in illicit sexual activity or stealing a few bucks from mother's purse. At the moment the action is performed, there is often little or no thought of actually doing something wrong. In fact, it may be seen as a very clever thing to do or a very exciting experience in which to indulge.

Later, when one is thinking a little more clearly and emotions have calmed down, the conscience is activated, logic takes over and guilt sets in.

"What was I thinking when I did that...stealing from my own mother?"

"How stupid to have gotten carried away last night! This is terrible."

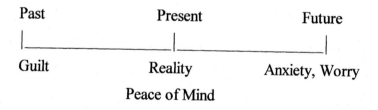

Past   Present   Future

Guilt   Reality   Anxiety, Worry

Peace of Mind

Guilt is now in command. Fear of punishment follows quite naturally. The key to resolve such conflicts is to remember that what is past no longer exists. Therefore, the guilt no longer exists! Nevertheless, guilt does continue to exist, but only in the mind, not in reality. What happened five minutes ago is gone forever. The only reality is the present moment. Are we then not guilty of anything we do, since the past does not exist? Oh, yes! We are still acting incorrectly and correction must be made. We are still responsible for our actions. Are we bad, evil and deserving of punishment? Not necessarily! The best correction would be to come to the realization that we are all one. We are not separate from God, family, friends or the church. There are rules of behavior to live by and we simply need to make proper forgiveness or correction.

How one makes corrections is established by each religion. Protestants will go to God directly; Catholics go to confession. If the offense can be resolved within oneself, that seems to be the preference of people today. For this reason, Catholics today are going to Communion—ninety-nine percent of them—without going to confession. This is a new phenomenon. Innocence and peace are being achieved in their minds, outside the usual procedure for Catholics seeking forgiveness. I am not making a judgment for or against this change in attitude. It is simply a common viewpoint today. Naturally, there is a small percentage of Catholics who still confess regularly.

While we are concentrating on guilt and its occurrence in the past, it would be appropriate to consider experiences that cause fear, fright and deep concern about a future that has not taken placed yet...and may never take place!

The fear of flying, a fear of darkness, possible earthquakes, the possibility of failing a test, are all anxieties about the future which have not yet taken place. Are they real? To the person having them...yes! Of course. Are they real in the present moment? No, not at all! They cannot be real, because the future has not happened yet. Only in the present moment is reality found. Since this is so, it is only in the present that we encounter God, speak to God, listen to God, relate to God. God is a God of the living, not of the dead or past, and not of the future which is not yet.

The conclusion from all this is to live in the *now moment*. That is where God's Peace, Joy and Happiness can be shared by us. That is where Heaven and Earth meet. That is where Creator and creature join as one. That is where you and I can find the greatest joy imaginable in this life.

4. THE NECESSITY OF CHANGE

All limitations are self-imposed.
—Ernest Holmes

It is a biological fact that anything that does not change is dead. The cells in our body, which are energy-in-motion, are always in a state of great activity. They are either growing, functioning or dying all the time. Organs, likewise, have work to do. They are not static, or, so to speak, *just sitting there* doing nothing. An organ, such as the heart or liver, would *atrophy* if it were not functioning. Larry, a very close friend and classmate—of happy memory—had that very problem with his heart. The back of the heart had atrophied; it was only a matter of time when his life would be cut short. His life ended soon after, and he was among the first of our class of 1956 to pass on.

Our minds cannot remain the same either, because the mind, too, is an energy, and energy can never remain dormant. Webster's New Collegiate Dictionary defines energy as the capacity of acting or being active, coming from the Greek word *energos*, meaning *at work, active, busy.* It will always find a way to express itself. Our minds are extremely active. It is estimated that more than 100,000 thoughts pass through our minds every day. We are not consciously aware of them, because we are protected from having to sort them out or giving consideration to each thought. In the same way, we are not aware of the blood circulating through our system, nor are we conscious of the food being broken down by our chemical factory of acids and enzymes and being converted into billions of fresh cells needed daily by the body.

If a person's mind is never challenged or awakened to new possibilities, it will run the same pattern of thoughts day after day. Again, if a person leads a very dull life with the repetition of the same activities every day, the thoughts may be compared to watching the same movie every day, over and over. I have witnessed this type of mind many times—thousands of times—while working in the inner city with *knights of the road* (street persons.) Since we had an Open Door Policy, the homeless, who walked the streets and slept at Rescue Missions, could come in without an appointment in order to receive some form of help. Many of them would give the same story of how they lost their job, their family and their security. Others would include how they started drinking. Usually, it was not their fault but caused by others. Even if it were their own fault, the story would be repeated each time with each visit.

I could predict, quite accurately, what some of them would

say, word for word. It is easy to get locked into a mind-set when there is not enough variation in a person's life. Just walking the streets every day and doing the same thing over and over does not allow the imagination to be exercised and retards the desire for change or challenge.

These thought-patterns are not restricted to the homeless. People with a good income, a steady job and a fine family can fall victim to the same kind of mind-set. If every day consists of work, food and television, and the only variation is the order in which they take place, there is the danger of falling into a mental trap. Just as our bodies need some exercise to function properly, so does the mind. Inducing the same thoughts each day is neither healthy, creative or exciting. I have discovered, in my years of counseling, that some marriages become quite dull and even depressing if nothing new is ever planned. Events will happen, of course, because life itself is unfolding, whether we like it or not. But we are co-creators with God! We need to be creative, exploring new ideas, making future plans or varying the activities by surprising one another with a gift, a ticket to see a play, suggesting an exciting place to go for a vacation or countless other possibilities.

It has become obvious to me that when you have a marriage in which one of the spouses is moving forward and the other is not, they tend to drift apart...sometimes leaving each other for good. Some spouses, to get out of the boredom of a dull life, start taking some courses in adult education. Regardless of what it may be: whether it is designed toward self-improvement in the form of painting or doing ceramics, or whether he or she joins a group that is studying some phase of metaphysics—the subject is not important—a couple can lose interest in each other, because, as we discussed earlier, one is living more creatively than before and communication begins to break down.

It is not enough just to tell a person what is wrong and why they are not communicating as they did previously. They need to be a part of the process. There must be a *change* in one's thinking, one's viewpoint, one's belief, one's attitude. This kind of change is called a *metanoia* from the Greek word meaning to change one's mind or one's heart. It refers to a radical change. Changes on the surface do not affect our thinking very much. Perhaps, temporarily, there will be a slight change, but after a brief period of time, one goes right back to where he or she started. We see this often with people who start something new, such as dieting, then give it up shortly. The desire for change has no depth. It is an empty desire and very soon, quite predictably, they proceed to put the weight back on again.

What is needed is a *radical* change that changes the whole person. It is swift and complete. A change at the level of "metanoia" even causes a *universal* healing within the person.

In this way, one's whole being experiences the change. Their close friends will notice immediately that this is not quite the same person who was always complaining about something, always angry at someone and either going to or coming from a fight. They will even say, "You look a little different. What did you do to yourself?" If you reduce your weight by fifteen or twenty pounds, their eyes pop out in amazement.

The key to a genuine radical change is education, meditation and the application of new principles by which to live. Education alone does not bring about the change desired. We know so little about ourselves, who we are, our origin, our purpose, our reason for living and our position in the Master Plan. There are very few persons on this earth with a perfect self-image. The Scriptures tell us a lot about ourselves and so do the sciences. In John 14:12, Jesus says: "I solemnly assure you, the one who has faith in me, will do the works that I do, and greater far than these." That is a powerful statement and promise. How many people do you know, who actually believe they can do what the Master Jesus did...and even greater things? What I am saying is: how many human beings believe they can walk on water, change water into wine or heal every sickness? And even *greater* things than those? If someone claims they can, I first want to see them walk on water (not ice) for starters!

The average self-image on this planet is far below what it really is. The general opinion of oneself is not even close to the truth. *God does not make junk. On the contrary, a human being is Nature's Masterpiece!* Unfortunately, that is not what the average person thinks. I had taught the Silva Method of Mind Development and Stress Control for fifteen years and part of the Course dealt with what constituted one's self image. After much discussion about this with many classes, it became obvious that the average persons's view of himself or herself is usually not only on the negative side, but often quite distorted.

I am not saying that *we are ready to walk on water!* But I am saying that there are certain facts about ourselves that, if put into practice, will put us on the right path that does lead to the truth of who we are and what we are capable of accomplishing in this life. The discovery of the true nature and make-up of a human being—without exception—helps tremendously in our development and self confidence. We will be able to face ourselves, our work, our families and the world with more wisdom and understanding—certainly, with a greater sense of peace and joy.

I have no intention of writing in profound terms, with its complicated sentences and hidden meanings. Rather, I have worked diligently at writing in simple, clear language. Understanding and comprehension are vital if we are serious about making a change in our life and our attitude. The grasp of happiness is just around the corner. My wish through this book is to help take you there. We are born with purpose; we live with purpose; we die with purpose. No one is born by accident. All that has ever happened before your birth prepared the world for your entry into this life.

5. DYING IS *REALLY* LIVING!

If you were going to die soon,
and you had only one phone call
you could make,
who would you call
and what would you say?
And why are you waiting?
                    —Stephen Levine

I was going to call this chapter, "Dying to Oneself Is *Really* Living!" That is quite true. I believe that when *we die to our lower self or ego, with its selfish attitude*, we begin to really live! That concept more or less runs through the whole book. Rather, I chose to reflect on the actual experience of physically dying momentarily and returning from what is called the near-death experience. A brief glimpse of our *true Home* changes lives permanently.

In everyday language, we speak of dying and going to heaven with the same impact as if we are *going Home*. We belong there because that is where we came from. We have a longing to return to where we started...our Eternal Home. In a way, there is a place in each of us, something like a *private altar*, where we meet God person to person and a decision is made, not by the family, not by the Church and not by the medical profession.

Karl Rahner is considered one of the greatest theologians of modern times. He is no longer with us, but he spoke of a *fundamental option* as the ultimate choice of a human being and forms the basis of life's direction as it unfolds...even as one is about to enter the world of spirit.

There are millions of Americans who have had the *near death* experience. In those situations, *decisions are not made alone.* They are able to talk to us about it because some person— usually a *being of light*—tells them that they still have work to do and are sent back into their bodies. They recover whether in the hospital with an illness that should have taken their life or, at times, even in the morgue. There are several documented cases of persons pronounced dead who were being readied in the morgue for burial—and shockingly returned to life, because their time had not come.

Jesus, of course, knew full well the circumstances of His death in advance and that He would rise again. He prayed that He would be spared the ill treatment He was to endure and the ignominious death on the cross, but He submitted to the Father's will. He was granted what no other person ever experienced! His was not a near-death experience. It was an actual death: a complete separation of body and spirit! He came back from the dead with a Risen and Glorified Body and remained for forty days with His followers, instructing them and preparing them to continue the work He had begun. After forty days, He became the Ascended Lord, a Universal Spirit Who is watching over us until the end of time, according to His promise.

We can speak, in a very real sense, of *returning* Home when we leave this world. We did have a Home in God. We were always an *idea* in the Mind of God. *When God has an idea, that idea is outside of time and space. It is eternal and will last forever.* We were created in the image and likeness of our Creator, not yesterday, not last week and not some fifty years ago, but *our spirit was created outside of time and space.*

There is a universal principle that *ideas never leave their source.* This is true of us also. Every idea we have ever had is locked up somewhere in our mind. A good hypnotist or therapist can help you to relive a past experience that is totally forgotten—even experiences going back to early childhood. Our conscious mind may not be aware of it, but everything we have ever experienced or learned is still recorded in the subconscious mind. This is also true of us who are prone to forget what we had for breakfast yesterday, or where we were on the tenth of last month—yet, it is all recorded—and if we are reminded of these facts the usual response is, "Oh, yes, now I remember!"

God's Mind is perfect. Nothing is ever forgotten. We are not forgotten! We have always been present in God's Mind and God's Life. When we leave this planet, we return Home where the average human being desires to be. Since we never left God, essentially, we journeyed without distance. We may be living out an experience and learning and discovering in this world, but we are also remembering, as we mature in spiritual wisdom, that our spirit has never left God.

Lest we forget, we are living in two worlds: the physical world and the spiritual world at the same time. Time tells us that we do not belong here forever. Our aging process reminds us daily. The average age of a human being keeps extending toward a ripe old age—at least in America. There are still some areas of the earth in which life is terminated quite early by comparison. No matter what medications or *secret formulas* are added to the new discovery list, we still are not destined, on an average, to spend more than a hundred years in our physical bodies. The only conclusion we can draw from our personal experience is, that we are *visitors* on this planet. *Pilgrims* passing through! *This is not our Home!* Yet, there is a tendency to make life here *our Home away from Home.* We can easily get caught up in the affairs of our social lives, our careers and our immediate goals, only to forget the spiritual reality of our existence. It is sad, indeed, when someone actually believes *this is all there is.* People everywhere are gaining a new insight. From what I see in the public forum, the news media and frequently, in the conversation among all classes of society, there is a rapidly growing concern about the reality of the *next life or afterlife.*

Bringing up the subject of the next step in human evolution, in which we will leave our bodies behind and move on, is no longer considered weird. I am not speaking of the traditional view of *dying, going to heaven and living happily ever after.* There are a lot more questions being asked today than ever before. I say this, not only because we have become a more educated society, but also because life itself is unveiling some of its larger truths. We have come to that significant level in human development, which is all-encompassing, universal and radical in its revelation.

While browsing in a Barnes and Noble store the other day, I noticed many books written by people from all walks of life who have had near-death experiences. It is not coincidental that these experiences are happening today with a growing frequency more than at any other time in history. Did they happen in the past? Of course they did! Did people talk about them? Probably not. It was rare indeed, but often we read of Saints who saw the *Land of Glory* before they left this world. The excitement of having a glimpse of their heavenly destiny or being greeted by a heavenly being of light was often witnessed by those in attendance. St. Bernadette of Lourdes, in France, had such an experience; she was greeted by the Mother of Jesus as she was making her transition to the edification and amazement of her attendant Sisters in the Religious life.

Bernadette, who was in a comatose condition, suddenly opened her eyes and smiled with unutterable joy as she was welcomed Home.

Today, people of all walks of life are talking about going through a tunnel, entering a land full of light. They are often met by *beings of light*. The place is a paradise with a dazzling environment filled with—and emanating—unconditional love and peace. Its attractiveness is impelling. One could hardly think of leaving such a happy state of mind. Yet, one by one, they are told that there is more work for them to do, and they must return to earth and complete the work assigned to them. Of course, there are many more who do not return to earth and begin their life in the spirit world.

How clearly these experiences emphasize *purpose* in life! The major events and circumstances in our life are not accidental. There is a *Master Plan!* We continue to make choices, of course, but the choices are made within a particular framework of our individual resolve and purpose.

Today, we are experiencing a new phenomenon in the medical field. People are revived more often as they enter death's door. Applying the Blue Code and shock treatments to flatliners (brain dead) are now accepted procedures. I have witnessed their work from time to time myself when called to anoint a dying patient. Some are revived and some are not! The survivors sometimes speak of floating above their own body and actually witnessing the doctors going through their ritual of maintaining life. In the past, the person in question would be called a *goner.*

Today every technique possible is used to revive a person who is dying. The medical field has truly revived many hopeless cases from actual death. Perhaps, that is one of the reasons why there are so many cases around the world of near-death experiences in our time. It is more a medical and natural phenomenon than a religious one. That is probably why it occurs in every country among every type of believer...or nonbeliever.

In a modern setting, with a new awareness, comes an additional enlightenment about afterlife. Those who "die" and return are never the same. They no longer fear death; they even welcome the death experience. *They know that life continues beyond the grave!* They become more spiritual; for them, life becomes more meaningful. That result should not be surprising. They entered the *world beyond, the afterlife, the next step, the secret passage of the ages.*

The lack of oxygen to the brain for just three minutes or longer leaves a person with brain damage—if they survive! This has always been an accepted medical fact. However, this is not the case with some of the near-death survivors. In some situations, the Natural Law is set aside in order to introduce a greater reality. Dr. George Ritchie, one of the most remarkable survivors who returned from the Land of Light, was considered dead for *nine* minutes. This case is fully documented. It was so extraordinary that he wrote an entire book—with full details—about that one experience. There was no brain damage! His brain functioned in a perfectly normal and healthy manner after his return from temporary death. This was a singular case, because it happened in 1943, long before it was fashionable or even considered possible to revive one who was brain-dead.

His book, *Return From Tomorrow,* is written simply, and is very exciting. It was hard to put down. Since he entered the world of spirit where there is no time or space, he tells of looking down at his own dead body and trying to communicate with those still in the flesh...making no headway. He speaks of meeting Christ, which was the highlight of all his extraordinary experiences on the other side of death. Since there is no *time* in spirit life, he had far more experiences than one would expect in a mere nine minutes. He became so accustomed to function without his physical body that, when he was looking for his body, he did not recognize it. Dr. Ritchie could not identify his own physical body—it had become so unnecessary to the experience of life he was enjoying. Finally, by looking more closely at the ring on the finger of one of the corpses, he realized—in shock—that what appeared to be so dull, lifeless and undesirable was the actual body he had to inhabit once again. It was not a happy moment! I highly recommend this book which has gone into its twenty-third printing.

Robert Grant is an author and a good friend of mine. In his book *Are We Listening to the Angels?*, he tells an incredible story about George Rodonaia a Russian professor and well-known scientist. He was considered dangerous because of his dissident activities and was assassinated by the KGB in 1975. His body was placed in deep freeze in the morgue. After three days, as the doctors were about to perform an autopsy on him, he suddenly revived. Brain damage should have been complete, leaving him in a totally unconscious state and totally incommunicable. Unbelievably, there was no brain damage! He entered the spirit world and returned with an entirely new perspective on life *here* and in the *hereafter*. He has been giving talks worldwide about his experience and also functions as an ordained Methodist Minister in Texas. In case you are wondering, this whole incident is well documented.

I was appointed Pastor of St. Michael's Church in Pontiac from 1972-77. It is located about a half-hour drive from downtown Detroit. The world famous Pontiac Motors headquarters is also located there. I enjoyed my Pastorate there very much. I loved the young and the old.

During those years in the seventies, it was a rewarding place to be. I especially endeared myself to the seniors organization which was called the *50-Up Club*. Actually, it was more like the *70-Up Club*. No matter! I loved to go to their meetings, their parties, and, occasionally, to their special celebrations during which I would participate in a few dances. I was impressed with the way they saw themselves, as younger rather than older. To tell the truth, I was younger in years, but I could not keep up with some of them.

One of the many wonderful parishioners I befriended was Helen Bateman. Though this incident happened over twenty years ago, I can remember it as if it were yesterday. Helen was always active in the church and was a daily communicant. (In the Catholic system, just going to church on weekends is not enough for many faithful Christians. There is a daily Mass or Religious service in every Parish. Their relationship with God is fostered daily through the official prayers of the Church and the reception of Communion.) I had about forty people attending daily Mass while I was in Pontiac. Helen was one of them. One day, her daughter Margie called to let me know that Helen was taken to the hospital and that she was comatose and dying. I dropped what I was doing and rushed to the hospital immediately! Her daughter was there waiting for me. When I arrived, Helen was in a comatose condition, and it was quite obvious that she was in the throes of death. My role was to give a dying person what, at that time, was called the Last Rites or Extreme Unction, both sounding like the final prayers before transition.

I arrived in good faith and performed the expected

Sacraments for the dying. However, since I was so familiar with Helen's active participation in St. Michael's Community and she was such a good friend to me, I decided to add my own spontaneous prayers. I began imploring God to restore her to sufficient health, so as to return home and to continue with her volunteer work in the St. Michael's Community. I sang her praises on how well she cooperated, how much she had accomplished and what wonderful things she was capable of doing upon her recovery to good health.

I was in the middle of this prolonged and complimentary prayer on Helen's behalf, when suddenly and surprisingly, she opened her eyes, looked at me straight in the eyes and yelled:

"Oh, shut up!!" She immediately went back into a coma. I then tried speaking to her as if she were awake, but I received no response whatsoever.

I looked across the bed at Margie and said, "We have to talk!" We stepped out into the hallway.

"I believe your mother wants to go Home. It is certainly obvious that she is looking for our approval to let her go and allow her to make her transition into the Heavenly Realms." Margie agreed, although it was certainly not an easy decision to make—concerning one's mother. We returned to her room. Margie and I, from both sides of the bed, held one of her hands.

I began humbly: "Helen, Margie and I are both sorry for misunderstanding your intentions. Please accept our blessing as you leave this world to fulfill your destiny. May the Lord bless you and protect you as you journey to heaven."

Helen suddenly came out of the coma again. She opened her eyes, looked at Margie, then looked at me and said, "Thank you!" to both of us, laid her head back and *expired at that very moment.* This time her desire was fulfilled.

I felt so much better having let her go. It was not my intention, nor the purpose of imparting prayers, nor the anointing to hold her back. The intention is a *healing* or a *safe passage* to the next life...in accord with God's Will.

The Catholic position regarding dying patients has indeed changed a lot since the seventies and our bedside manner has become more compassionate and more in keeping with current procedure as *care givers* to those whose health and life are considered terminal. In fact, the former Last Rites is now called *The Anointing of the Sick.* Through the years, so many incredible healings and recoveries have been witnessed. Today, anything is possible!

Yet, I was never prepared for this. A person comes out of a coma, not once, but twice to give those present a very important message: "Let me go! Please! It's my time, and I am ready!" I had never had that experience before. It went beyond my scope of knowledge and experience. I do not believe that anything in Medical Science could have helped either. These unusual circumstances may never happen again in my life time, but I shall always be grateful for knowing the importance of letting go of our loved ones, who after finishing their mission on earth, want to move on.

I had another experience at St. Joseph's Hospital in Pontiac, not long after visiting Helen Bateman. I do not recall the name of the other lady since she was not active at St. Michael's Church—only because she was quite elderly by the time I was assigned there.

I rushed to the hospital after receiving the call for a priest. When I arrived, there were six or seven family members gathered around the bed. They were all in tears, while I was blessing her with the Anointing of the Sick. She was totally unconscious during the entire time I was giving her the Sacrament. When I finished, I was about to leave, when suddenly, she opened her eyes and spoke for the first time in several days. She was facing the wall, not us, as this conversation that took place.

"Am I supposed to die now or what?" There was silence for a few moments. We heard nothing, but she was listening attentively.

"I can't make that decision. I thought God decided those things!" Silence, again.

"I really don't know. What does God think?" Once more there was a silence.

"Oh! Well, that is what I want also. If that is God's will,

then I am ready!" Those were her last words. She died at that very moment.

We were all stunned, but that is exactly what happened!

I did a lot of thinking after that experience. *Is the moment of death interactive? Do we have a choice? Is it an option? Is it a shared experience between creature and Creator?* I had a lot more questions than answers. And still do! I have been told of many cases in which the dying person would not die until a spouse, a son or daughter or a very close friend arrived. This is not always true, obviously. My nephew, Bob Rashid simply collapsed and died on the golf course recently. There was no specific warning! His wife and three children were confronted with a totally unexpected tragedy. Their whole life was radically changed in a moment of time. In Bob's particular transition, there was no interactive experience with the Lord of Life—unless a contract was made long before his time to move on.

Again, we are confronted with the mystery of death. Once we are born into this world, an unbreakable commitment is established. No one is immune to the experience of passing over to the world of spirit—invisible to the physical eye. How, when or under what circumstances it will take place, is hidden from us so that we can live our lives normally from day to day. The only two exceptions in human history that I know of are Elijah and the mother of Jesus. As far as you and I are concerned, I wouldn't count on it happening to us...we *know neither the day nor the hour...*

6. DEATH: THE ULTIMATE EXPERIENCE

Death is one of two things.
Either, it is annihilation
and the dead have no consciousness of anything;
or, as we are told, it is really a change:
a migration of the soul from this place to another.

—Socrates

Death is described by a great teacher of our time as an explosive, magnificent experience, topping anything we have ever experienced before. Those who have had near-death experiences testify to this. In fact, they are so deeply impressed with *a temporary death*—which may have lasted only a few moments or minutes—that they are no longer afraid to die. This is a universal response.

About ten years ago, I visited a man in a hospital in the Detroit area, who *died* several times. His heart stopped each time. He was clinically dead! Code Blue was applied and he recovered consciousness each time. He maintained that a *spirit helper* visited him each time and assured him he would not die. However, since he, to all appearances, "died" each time, his family was called in. They came each time—five or six times—

expecting their father to pass on to the next world. He was delighted that his children dropped everything to comfort him, but he maintained he would be told by the spirit guide, exactly when he would *actually* make his transition. A few days later, he told his children to see him on a certain day. It would be his last. According to his final wishes, the whole family was present. He said his *good-byes* to each of his seven grown children and related to them how he wanted his possessions divided among them. At a certain moment, he said he was being visited by a spirit guide who was telling him it was time to go...and he died. *This time he really died!* He made his final exit right on schedule! I walked out of the hospital wondering about death. Just what do we know about the moment we are born and the moment we die? I was affirmed in my own belief that *our death is already known perfectly well in advance.*

This topic is larger than just the moment of death. There is Divine Guidance and direction being given continually...in every circumstance! It is our own lack of awareness that prevents us from recognizing the *Hand of God* in our daily actions...*and in our final exit.* I have related a great deal about my spiritual and mystical experiences through the years. Exactly how they affected me is hard to put into words. Each experience *raised more questions than I was able to answer adequately.* How could anyone be well enough prepared—back in the forties and fifties—to comprehend the unknown and the mystical? That was the period of time before the space age, computers and talk of near-death experiences. There was still a dark veil covering the evidence of a larger picture of truth, limiting our view of unseen realities in matters encompassing the spiritual, medical and scientific fields of knowledge. My entire educational background, beginning with the primary grades, right up to my ordination to the priesthood, could not possibly have been sufficient preparation to foresee the incredible and unbelievable experiences that were placed in my path.

I still pause in silence and wonderment at how I was encouraged by the Voice of Holy Spirit (or one of the Spirit's Helpers) to enter the Seminary, how I was guided by the Spirit into unknown territories of reality—and how the results affirmed the authenticity of my experiences. All this is described in detail in my first book: *On My Way Home.*

Two other people I have known very well in my life have contributed to a radical change in my views about the moment of death—more specifically, what happens immediately upon leaving the body.

The first was in 1980 when my sister Marie made her passing into eternal life. She was at Beaumont Hospital in a suburb just north of Detroit. She went in to have a check-up for a very painful back. She could get no rest, nor any relief from the pain. I was urged to go to the hospital since, as I was told, her condition had become serious. While I was changing shirts from a casual one to my clerical shirt, my face and bare arms suddenly felt as if someone was gently touching me—more like embracing me—causing the hair on my arms to stand straight out! Even the hair on my head did the same. I immediately thought of my sister Marie making her transition. I checked my watch. It was 12:32 pm. There was no doubt in my mind. She gave me a *hug* to say goodbye as she made her way to her next level in the afterlife. I offered a prayer to bid her farewell...till we meet again!

When I arrived at the hospital, I was met in the hallway by my sister Lillian and my Aunt Billie, my mother's youngest sister. Before they had a chance to say anything to me, I said simply and sadly, "She died at 12:32 pm. I know. I believe she visited me."

They looked at their watches, quite shocked that I knew, but also quite relieved that they did not have to break the awful news to me. They, then, explained to me that Marie was preparing to return home, since they found nothing particularly wrong with her. While she was getting ready she was speaking to her son George, calling him Bill (the name of her deceased husband). Then she stopped abruptly in the middle of a sentence and expired! It took quite a while to get over her death, but the one consolation that helped me through it was that *she said goodbye to me on her final passage Home.*

I do not remember reading anywhere that spirits leaving their bodies, can take the time and effort to say goodbye to people. I was deeply moved that she contacted me before moving on. (I had another visit from her since then.)

In 1983, another incident added to my amazement about people dying and leaving evidence that they wished to say farewell at the time of their *departure*. It was August 15, the Feast of the Assumption of Jesus' Mother into heaven. It was lunchtime again and we always had visitors for lunch. That time we had a few extra guests because of the Holy Day. Fr. Clement Kern had been in an accident on the freeway several weeks before and was slowly recovering. At least, I thought he was. While the ten of us were in the middle of the meal, the grandfather clock began to chime. It surprised us all, since the clock had not worked in years. (I had the same feeling I did when my sister died.) Fr. Kern made his passing known to us, as he made his way to the Heavenly Kingdom. I had to ask if anyone present had gotten the big clock fixed recently. No one, apparently, had touched it.

After the funeral, Mr. Archer, one of the many benefactors of Most Holy Trinity Church, upon hearing the story about the clock, offered to have the clock repaired, at his cost. We found a man who specialized in repairing old grandfather clocks. He checked it over very thoroughly and made it clear to me that *there was no way that this clock could have chimed. Also, that the essential parts to make the clock work and to chime were missing or broken.* In fact, even if it were working, it would be impossible to chime off the regular hour on the hour. He reiterated, as he was leaving, that it was literally impossible for the clock to work or to chime. Yet, all ten of us heard it at exactly 12:47 p.m.! Shortly after, we received a phone call that Fr. Kern had died. We were not surprised.

It is quite exciting when someone we know says goodbye, either in words or by their actions, at the point when they are ready to go Home. *It is also encouraging to know that they are still alive and well!* The authentic witness of so many people causes us to pause for a moment and to reconsider more profoundly our childhood beliefs—in contrast to our present and critical viewpoint as mature adults.

I used to tell my students when I was teaching Metaphysics, "Don't be afraid of death! You'll *live* through it!" I believe that even more so today! Actually, death is not an end, but a beginning, a new birth into the realm of spirit. One of the comforting elements of death is that we have completed our task, and our purpose for being here has been accomplished. We made it! We graduated! It's time to move on to the next level of life to the grand, mysterious, multi-layered dimensions of Reality.

In heaven or the spirit world, there will be one big difference compared to life on earth. After leaving *this mortal coil*, as Shakespeare would say, there is no longer the lapse of time between what we desire and what becomes our reality. Whatever we choose or desire is our reality...immediately! Why is this so? Because there is no time in the spirit world. All things are *now*!

We can only get a *glimpse* of living in a timeless situation while still in this physical world. Watching a really exciting movie, in which we are fully engrossed and captivated, removes the sense of time. We feel as if the two hours were just a few minutes. Also, deep meditation takes us into a state of mind that is beyond time and space. Years ago, while I was in Puerto Rico studying Spanish and Hispanic Culture, I was walking past the chapel and I noticed a pair of shoes on the floor outside the door. I looked inside to see if they belonged to someone inside the chapel. Sitting on the floor in a full lotus position (a difficult yoga posture) directly in front of the altar was the director of the program I was attending. I noticed an alarm clock at his side while he meditated. Later that day, I asked him about the clock. He told me that when he meditates, he becomes completely oblivious of time. In other words, he could sit there meditating for one hour, two hours, five hours or more, but his busy life did not allow him that much luxury of time. For him, time did not exist during the altered states of awareness.

Circumstances, other than praying or meditating can produce a similar result. They may not take us into the higher realms of consciousness, but they can distract us from the minutes and even the hours passing by. Enjoying a party or a wedding reception can have the same result, if we are with relatives and close friends we haven't seen in a long time. The evening goes by in a flash. These are only momentary occasions. Imagine living in a world where we are never aware of minutes, hours and days, because there is no sun-time. The light, provided in the world of spirit is the continuous and never-ending Eternal Light that emanates from God's Presence!

In the timelessness of the spirit world, a *thousand earth years* will seem like a *moment*. While History is being made in this world and we live through it every day with countless experiences, persons in the spirit world see a much larger picture in one glance. That is why the *past, present and future* are going on at the same time in the next life. They can see into *our* future because *there is no future!* Only the present moment, the Eternal Now, exists in God's World. Not only does God know our so-called future, but even our relatives who have passed on know quite well what is going to happen to us in the world of time. Some people, who are psychic in this life, can tap into the mental and spiritual dimensions of reality, foretelling the future...and quite accurately. President John Kennedy received ample warnings from psychics all over the nation about going to Dallas that unforgettable day. His destiny, however, dominated the occasion. He could have at least used the special vehicle with the bullet-proof bubble, just in case the psychics were correct. His manner of making his transition was bigger than life!

Describing a world without time in which the past, present and future are wrapped into one, sounds like a place where all our dreams are fulfilled rather quickly. That is true! In the world of spirit, whatever we *imagine* to be real is *real* to us! We can imagine or desire to have a nice job, live in a comfortable home, have a television set in every room, enjoy a wonderful family and live happily ever after. Sooner or later, however, we will have to come to the conclusion that we are out of touch with Reality, and our enjoyment of that *ideal life* will get boring...or at least, unreal. We cannot be eternally happy living separate lives, behind separate walls that keep us from each other.

The truth is, as the Master Jesus reminds us, we are neither married nor given in marriage in the life to come, but rather, we shall be like angels. There is no marriage in heaven, since there is *no need to reproduce* by having children. This changes our whole perspective concerning the sexual differences between male and female.

Just being in the spirit world, also changes our values. Television would no longer be necessary. Subconscious minds communicate directly. It should not be surprising to you that the average American spends twenty-six hours watching television each week. Wouldn't you call that an addiction or an obsession? Also, the time and energy spent on dedication to sports, money, work, hobbies or the Internet has replaced our devotion to God in many ways. Whether they are idols or not, they are the sources that are feeding our minds every day...almost hypnotically. As I previously mentioned, when we enter God's World, our *values* become altered radically! It will be a shocking experience to know that our minds and spirits are all united in God as *one,* even though we keep our *individuality.* Heaven is a relationship with our Source! Our higher minds are united here on earth also but not our conscious minds. Carl Jung speaks of the collective unconscious, referring to that hidden subconscious/superconscious mind within us. We think, act, and believe separately in this world. The *conscious* mind or *ego* does not want anyone to interfere with its privacy. In fact, we are offended when someone is trying to tell us what to believe and we have a completely opposite opinion. In the spirit world, truth will be shared by those who are open to it. We merely need to desire information, and it is immediately known—without separate lives, in separate little houses, with separate incomes and expenses. We will no longer be struggling *to make ends meet.*

We shall enter the spiritual realm where all others in that realm (mansion) share the same values. In the next world, just as in this world, *like attracts like!* This is a Universal Principle! People gravitate to persons with whom they can communicate. They will spend hours together enjoying the fact that there is someone in this world who is actually listening to them and understands the point they are trying to make. However, from a purely physical point of view, *opposites attract.* Many marriages take place because there is an extraordinary physical attraction—which is fine! Unfortunately, as many couples have discovered, problems begin to surface when there is a conflict in spiritual values, convictions or style of living. If there is little attraction on the spiritual and mental levels of communication, the fragile and purely physical bond holding them together is not enough—especially in later years when physical attraction diminishes or is completely gone on the part of one or both spouses.

Some folks have a false impression of the next life. We are *not transformed into perfect beings* as soon as we leave our physical bodies. We are still the same—with our individual attitudes, weaknesses, strengths and beliefs. There are many advantages in the afterlife, but we are basically still ourselves. There will be little spiritual enlightenment for those who were hardened criminals or evil-minded souls here on earth. If they persist in their false belief of separation and selfishness or continue to take whatever they can out of life without care or concern about others, they will find themselves in the realm of like minds...since like attract like! Their need is to learn some fundamental lessons on proper behavior and the reality of some basic truths...*if they so desire!* There will be *no force!* Those souls, who persist in their belief in separation and continue to live by earthly and selfish principles, will find themselves in dark realms far from reality of God's Presence. Their position may be described as *hellish*. It is the result of their own choices. Although it is close to our images of hell, there is one difference. *There is a way out!*

It is time to revisit our previous interpretations of the concept of hell. Do I believe in hell? Yes, I certainly do. Do I believe it is a divided spirit world where there is separation into three dimensions, like a three-layered cake, with heaven above, purgatory in the middle and hell below—three separate realms? I don't think so! My answer needs some clarification! First of all, you cannot divide spirit. All is *one,* even though we are still *individuals,* like *drops of water* in the ocean. Are there many realms or mansions in the spirit world? Yes, Jesus assured us of that! I would further extend the same three areas into realms of *relationship* that are differentiated by Eternal Light and Truth, as mentioned above. The words of Jesus are interesting, "In my Father's House there are many mansions." *Mansions* are generally seen as levels of awareness, realms of enlightenment or states of consciousness.

The ultimate goal or achievement of Creation is that all souls, without exception, will be of one Mind in God's Kingdom, the Original State in which we, God's family, were created. St. Paul (1 Corinthians 15:22-28) gives us a convincing argument when he declares that:

Just as in Adam all die, so in Christ all will come to life again, but each one in proper order: Christ, the first fruits, and then, at His coming, all those who belong to Him. After that, will come the end, when after having destroyed *every sovereignty, authority, and power,* He will hand over the Kingdom to God the Father. Christ must reign until God has put *all* enemies under His feet, and the last enemy to be destroyed is death. Scripture reads that "God has placed all things under His feet." But when it says that *everything* has been made subject, it is clear that He (God) Who has made everything subject to Christ is excluded. When finally, *all* has been subjected to the Son, He will subject Himself to the One who made *all things subject to Him*, so that God may be *all in all*.

In the Seminary, one of our professors maintained that in heaven we will all be filled to our capacity with God's Love, but we all differ in capacity through our experience and application of unconditional love. This is an opinion that has some logic to it. As an example, even though we are all *created* equal, as recorded in the Sacred Scriptures and affirmed by President Lincoln in his Gettysburg address, we are not, however, *born* equal. This is evident in many ways: some babies come into this world as a child of a powerful Royal Family, others are born in a ghetto or a refugee camp. Of course, there are still others born healthy into an average family, while other babies come into this world physically challenged with AIDS, encephalitis or any number of infant diseases. Even if we are born in rather equal surroundings in the same country and in the same neighborhood, *each of us still choose our separate way of life*. Few people on the earth, at this time, would place themselves side by side with the accomplishments of Mother Teresa or other great souls for their outstanding achievements in human history. Nevertheless, in due time...we shall all be happy.

PART TWO

One of the first conflicts I encountered as a youngster was the image of God I was *taught* as a child and the Reality of God that I was *actually experiencing*. There was, literally, a world of difference. In the primary grades and in the Seminary, I seemed to become more and more conscious of sin, rather than of God's Love. The image of God, as described by authorities somehow conveyed a god who was the punisher, who knew every thought I had—good or bad—and was ready to pronounce judgment on me at any moment. The God I learned about caused accidents, sickness and death at random; he was a disciplinarian. My classmates shared these same views, whenever we discussed our relationship to God. Such frightening images made a deep impression on my young mind, in spite of a more loving picture of God I received from my parents. Also, I am not sure about other priests, but I do remember, from my altar boy days that Fr. Ferdinand DeCneudt in his sermons, always presented a God Who was loving, fatherly and approachable—and quick to forgive. Nevertheless, in my little mind, the *negative* view of God somehow seemed to take hold more than the *positive*. Why not? I believed, in those days, that if I even ate a piece of meat on any Friday, I was going to hell forever!

In the following chapters, I address our relationship to God and how we are all united to one another in God. I spend no time in painting a picture of a god—as many still believe—that is much too small to run a world or, better yet, a whole Universe. It is truly amazing to know that there are great numbers of sincere people who still carry some pretty warped ideas about the Perfect, Infinite, All-Powerful, Loving Creator Who has no equal in the Universe...and I am not excusing myself. I was one of them!

I appreciate God's magnitude a lot more today than I did in the past, but the revelation and understanding of the *Infinite* never ends...

7. MY RESPONSE TO GOD'S GRACE

I fled Him down the nights and down the days;
I fled Him down the arches of the years;
I fled Him down the labyrinthine ways
of my own mind; and in the midst of tears
I hid from Him, and under running laughter.

—Francis Thompson

As far back as I can remember, there was never a time when God seemed totally distant. Whether things were going well or not, I still remembered that God was present and had something to do with what was happening. I have been through some ugly situations and also a few devastating ones. Regardless of how horrible the circumstances may have been, it was still relatively easy for me to remember God's Presence, even if it were merely an opportunity to blame God for my problems. As I grew spiritually, I began to realize that God has never been the cause of my unhappiness...nor could He be. God, by His very Nature, wishes only the best for His children. My early life at home with the family had a lot to do with my image of God. We often spoke of God in ordinary conversation. God was always a part of our lives. It was, and still is, a common practice among Arabic-speaking people. For instance, in my early home life, we rarely ever used such expressions as, *"Good luck", "Hope all goes well", "Have a safe trip!"* and so on.

Rather, we would say "Allah maek", meaning *God be with you.* (The English letters transliterate directly from the Arabic. I am not sure how to spell these Arabic words, so any incorrect use of English phonetics is my error. And thanks to Tony Abou-Dib who helped me with the Arabic.)

Another expression frequently used was "Nishkur Allah!" or *Thank God!* Heard just as often is the familiar expression: "Inshallah" or *God willing!* Anytime we were saying goodbye to a relative or friend, or planning a trip, hoping to arrive at one's destination or to return safely, Inshallah was used. In desperate situations, my mother always looked up to the Heavens, crying out, "Ya Rubbee!" Translated, *Oh, God!* —meaning, I need help!

When suddenly confronted with a frightening situation, my parents would cry out: "Ismus saleeb," or *In the name of the Cross (of Christ, may I be protected!.)* If someone died the usual statement was "Allah yer hamoo." If it were a female that died, the last word would be the feminine form: "hama." I have a plaque in my home which says, "Hedde min fadl Rubbee!" Freely put in English, would be: *"All I have is from the generosity of God."*

It is plain to see that I came from a culture that was God-conscious. Not only was the existence of God taken for granted, but the Presence of God was a *Reality* and not just an intellectual *concept*. Nothing was left to chance! God was very much involved in our daily lives, our daily activities, our jobs, our families, our country, our purposes in life, our troubles, our celebrations and so forth. Our relationship to God was everything!

Nevertheless, when I reflect on my pursuit of truth and my relationship to God, I realize it was not all that simple. Being involved in multiple situations that challenged my faith and trust in the Lord, Who showered me with gifts, I still found it hard to accept the invitation of a Divine Being who made Himself known, but not seen. The seed of faith must be watered and nurtured until at some point, we make a *leap of faith* that rises to another level. As our view of reality broadens, we can without any doubt, finally come to the conclusion that Christ was always drawing us to Himself. It was a hard lesson to learn: *We are never abandoned!* On the contrary, it is He who tracks us down like a hunter...and finally brings us to our knees—in prayer.

Perhaps, then, you can identify with my personal experience with the Divine Hunter Who would not give up on me, even when I was on the edge of giving up on myself. One day, in meditation, the following words poured out of me. It was mostly inspired by the very experiences I was having, but did not understand fully:

Since I was a child
I have always felt His Presence.
It was the presence of a Pursuer
seeking His prey. And I prayed!

I questioned my experiences.
Were they just wild imaginings;
or did the dreams, visions,
and mystical experiences really happen?

The human mind challenges
anything out of the ordinary.
But there was always evidence in my path!
Did Someone care that much about me?

As time moved on...so did my Pursuer!
I thought He would give up.
He said He would never stop
as long as I kept running...

And running I did. I hid...it did me no good!
He was always there, waiting with arms outstretched:
"You have nothing to fear, My son,
I am with you through every dark moment on your path."

No one can keep up this pace.
The chase would surely end soon.
But no, not this Pursuer. He would not let me go.
Did He know things about me that I did not know?

I paused: Can there be a thought without a Source?
Do not all flowers have roots?
How could I be so blind as to think
I just came to be...quite by accident!

Yet, I continued to run, even gallop,
no longer moving in a straight line,
missing every turn and tripping often,
but there He was: that Voice that wouldn't stop.

When I was down and all seemed lost,
He said to me again,
"You have nothing to fear, My son,
Simply take hold of my hand."

I took a step forward feeling very awkward
in territory unfamiliar.
Then my step seemed to widen. I leaped!
And what a joy! What a beautiful world I began to see.

Beyond the eyes, beyond the veil, the view is magnificent.
I could see with clarity what really is.
The truth is all-encompassing!
Nothing is less than what it should be.

Whenever the thought of the past emerges
and I feel drawn to the world of sleep, He reminds me:
"You have nothing to fear, My son,
what is, will always be."

8. WE ARE ALL ONE

Every human action, mental or otherwise,
takes place in the context of relatedness.

—Diarmuid O'Murchu

"Good evening, friend. What are you doing?"
"I am throwing these starfish back in the ocean.
If I don't, they'll die here on the sand."
"There must be thousands of starfish on this beach.
You can't possibly save them all.
You can't possibly make a difference."
He smiled, picked up yet another starfish
and threw it into the sea.
"It made a difference to that one!"

—Mark Hansen and Jack Canfield (adapted)

Calling a friend on the phone makes us feel quite close to the party on the other end of the line, but talking to God is infinitely closer and more important. How do I know that Almighty God is listening to my prayer among the millions of prayers going on all the time? God listens to every prayer at the same time, because we are never really separate from God.

Most of us are caught into a thought pattern that everything is separate. We are all on our own. Why not? Our environment testifies to that situation. We all live in different homes, own different cars, have our own line of work and have our own set of problems. No one else is going to take care of our bills, pay our rent or buy groceries for us. Those actions are separate, and to all appearances, *everything* and *everyone* is separate from every other! *"You take care of your life; I take care of mine!"* That is commonly believed.

Statistics betray us by emphasizing our separateness. The following was given to me on April 19, 1999. If we could shrink the earth's population to a village of precisely 100 people, with all the existing human ratios remaining the same, it would look like this:

> 57 Asians,
>
> 21 Europeans,
>
> 14 from the Western Hemisphere,
>
> > (North and South America)
>
> 8 Africans,
>
> 52 would be female,
>
> 48 would be male,
>
> 70 would be non-white,
>
> 30 white,
>
> 70 would be non-Christians,
>
> 30 would be Christians,
>
> 89 would be heterosexual,
>
> 11 homosexual,

59 % of the entire world's wealth would be in the
hands of only six people and all six would be
citizens of the United states,

80 would live in substandard housing,

70 would be unable to read,

50 would suffer from malnutrition,

1 would be near death,

1 would be near birth,

1 would have college education and

1 would own a computer.

From all external measurements and human logic, it would seem quite clear that we live in a terribly unfair, dysfunctional, unjust and unreasonable world in which the distribution of wealth, territory, education and the standard of living are a disgrace. Everybody and everything appear totally separate. And granted, *it is a disgrace*! Yet the thought of each person being completely separate from everyone else is the *greatest lie* ever to confront the human mind!

The truth is that we are all one and I am not speaking in figurative language! Regardless of appearances, I still affirm that we are one. In fact, in the *grandest order* of things, we are remarkably more united than separate. Spiritually, we are all one. We cannot separate *spirit;* We cannot divide it, break it up into little pieces, cut it or destroy it. Spirit is indivisible. Spirit is one! Since we were created pure spirit by Divine Spirit, we too, essentially, are spirit. Although spirit, by its very nature, cannot be divided and we are many, none of us lose our *identity* while sharing the same Spirit of Life...God's Spirit. Outside of God, there is no life! St. Peter grasped this idea when he said that through the gifts God gave us, we become sharers in the Divine Nature. Many songs are written with that same theme, such as: "We are one in the Spirit, we are one in the Lord..."

Ask a young child: "Where is God?" Without hesitation, the child will answer, "God is everywhere!"

If we open our eyes and observe closely, an ocean can be seen as *one body of water* or it can be considered an accumulation of *millions and millions of drops of water.*

We are all familiar with St. Paul's beautiful analogy of being one in the Spirit, by considering the human body and its composition of many parts, as found in 1 Corinthians: 12-28:

> The body is one and has many members, but all the members, many though they are, are one body. If the foot should say, "Because I am not a hand, I do not belong to the body," would it, then, no longer belong to the body? If the ear should say, "Because I am not an eye, I do not belong to the body," would it then no longer belong to the body? If the body were

all eye, what would happen to our hearing? If it were all ear, what would happen to our smelling? As it is, God has set each member of the body in the place He wanted it to be. There are, indeed, many members, but one body...even the members of the body which seem less important are, in fact, indispensable. If one member suffers, all the members suffer with it; if one member is honored, all the members share its joy. You then are the body of Christ. Everyone of you is a member of it.

Our bodies are an amazing phenomenon. They are nothing short of miraculous when they are viewed as organisms made up of many millions of individual cells. The actual composition of our bodies is startling! According to the American Biologist, Dr. Hudson Hoagland, there are about *500 billion cells that die every day* and are replaced with new ones. This should not cause anyone to worry or to lose any sleep. Our bodies are made up of about 60,000 billion cells!

An interesting corollary to this, is that since energy cannot be destroyed, the billions of cells that die each day are changed back into their basic building blocks of atoms and molecules. These same atoms are converted into the food that become part of the cells in another person's body or the atoms of one person are inhaled by another. Scientifically, we can say that we are swapping atoms all the time! Extending this concept even further, we can actually say that we all share, to some degree, some of the atoms that made up the body of Jesus two thousand years ago, including the body of Moses, Abraham Lincoln or Mother Teresa.

When we ask the question: Are we also connected physically? Very much so! Our bodies are continually renewing themselves. The composition of the human body is mostly liquid. Dr. Rudolph Schoenheimer, an authority in this field, stated that "all constituents of living matter, whether functional or structural, are in a steady state of rapid flux." Our bodies are mostly composed of liquids in constant circulation, so that our chemical factory (under the direction of the subconscious mind) can change the great variety of food we eat into new and exact molecules that make up the different nerves, tissues, muscle, blood, brain cells, etc.

The British authority, Sir Charles Dodds, affirms that in the human body, "the total turnover of proteins occurs in about 80 days, while the liver and serum proteins were turned over in 10 days and the lung, brain, bone, skin and principle muscle in 158 days.

To put it in another way, when we meet a friend we have not seen for about six months, we will recognize that friend immediately, even though *all the protein that makes up his or her face has been changed and there is not one molecule in it that was there* when we last saw that person. This is true of every human being...of everything that is alive. Although the cells that make up our bodies change frequently, changes in appearance—what we look like to others—take place rather slowly as we age with time.

Our minds, of course, are also joined together. There is only one mind...God's Mind! Again, we simply share in the Mind of God. We are generally not aware of this fact at all. Later, my reflections will center on the purpose and power of meditation and the exhortation of St. Paul to "put on the Mind of Christ." We will also explore, in another chapter, the three aspects of the human mind: the conscious, the subconscious and the superconscious mind.

In a practical way, we do recognize our oneness. Witnessing, for example, an accident, we immediately feel terrible about what happened to a friend, relative or even a total stranger. When someone dies, the sorrow is felt by everyone: "Too bad! She was such a nice person," or "Can you imagine? Cut off so early in life?" These are average, normal comments we often hear.

And it is quite appropriate to show compassion and concern for others in distant lands. We may not sense it consciously, but we feel bonded to those who meet an untimely death, even though we have never crossed paths in this life—and never will! Take, for example, the news on August 9,

1998, that eleven Americans were killed when two American Embassies were blown up at the same time, senselessly killing so many employees. Around the same time, others were killed in the Sudan...or in China from a horrible earthquake and floods. Being connected, we feel their pain...thousands of families grieving over other members of the human family we never have, nor ever will meet in our lifetime.

We are all in this together!

What we don't realize is that *there is another side to everything* that takes place in our lives or in the lives of those around us. We are slow to comprehend that there are purposes being fulfilled at every moment. There are reasons for everything that has an impact on our life. *We are here to experience and through those experiences to remember who we are and our relationship to our Creator.* This is the purpose of human life. There are no accidents! How could there possibly be *accidents* with an All-knowing, Infinite Being who has Perfect Knowledge of all things...which unfold in our experience as past, present and future.

Jesus says that even the hairs on our head are numbered by the Lord; that every tiny sparrow that falls to the ground is known by God; that the flowers in the field are decorated by the Lord to the point of being more beautiful than Solomon in all his royal robes. And that God does not take time off, neither on weekends nor holidays. "My Father goes on working..."

Nothing escapes the Mind of the Creator!

Yes, God sees all life, all forms of life in all places at one and the same time. There is only one Source and everything is related to that Source. So why shouldn't there be communication on all levels among all forms of life. After all, *God's children are all connected in mind and spirit—and in body, through atoms which are interchanged all the time.*

I had a personal experience of our connectedness one day while driving to Warren, Michigan, to visit my sisters. I was on the freeway, when I suddenly got off at the wrong exit. It was raining furiously and I could not see well in front of me. I became confused when I came off the ramp; I decided I had to go a little further to get back on the freeway.

Again, I made another wrong turn. Now, I found myself very close to Mt. Olivet Cemetery. It was still raining hard. I decided that instead of going back on the freeway, in what was almost a rainstorm, I would enter the cemetery and visit my parents' graves...if I could find them. I had not gone to visit their graves in almost two years before that day. There I was, with the wind and rain blowing furiously, getting all wet, and looking for their graves which were never easy to find.

I finally began to give up! There was no way I could find their graves. And I was not going to go to the front office to find the exact location and all the way back again! Frustrated, I started back to the car. In desperation, I happened to look down one last time...at a grave, just before stepping over it. I was stunned! There was my mother's grave right in front of me. I thought for a moment...why am I standing here in the rain, getting all wet, at this time? Then the thought became a flash of light! *This is the anniversary of my mother's death—her twenty-fifth anniversary!* I prayed in tears...then got back on the road.

Death itself is unable to separate us. We remain connected as one; even time and space cannot break the bond.

9. WHERE IS GOD
WHEN WE ASK FOR HELP?

We turn to God for help when
our foundation is shaking,
only to recognize that
it is God who is shaking it.
—Charles Weston

Just where is God when we need Him? Right where we would expect: fully present, knowing exactly where we are, sending us His constant Love, watching over our loved ones and often responding to our prayers and needs even before we ask. God is aware of our every thought, every problem, real or imagined, and helps us in surprisingly, wondrous ways. He has many helpers, in this world and in the next, who actively come to our aid. I can testify from experience to this.

Here is one example...it was 1976. While stationed at St. Michael's Church in Pontiac, Michigan, something most unusual happened, which made a profound impact on my life. To this very day, I am still grateful for the experience.

What occurred took place two nights in succession. The first night I was awakened abruptly and realized that I had received a visitation from a person who was from the spirit world. When you can see a person clearly, and, at the same time, see *through* that person, you know immediately that you are in the presence of a spirit-being. That's the way it occurs to me.

It was about 4:00 a.m. when I was awakened. A spirit-being was standing in front of my bed.. I had no idea who he was.

I said: "Who are you?" No response!

"Why are you here?" Again, he did not speak! I did not give up asking.

"What do you want?" He still did not reply. I said "If you are evil, begone in the name of Christ!" He did not leave...nor did he speak. It may sound strange, but I was genuinely tired—so I simply went back to sleep.

The very next night I was awakened about the same time, while I was sound sleep. I slowly opened my eyes and there was the same person who visited me the night before.

"Oh, it's you again!" I said. "Are you going to just stand there or are you going to speak to me this time?" This time I spoke more boldly.

After a moment of silence, he did speak, "Do you know who I am?"

"No!" I answered. "I have never seen you before."

Then he gave me his name! I responded that there is no way that you could be that person. Years ago, at the Trappist

Monastery, called Gethsemani, in Bardstown, Kentucky, I had seen the person he claimed to be, from a distance. The person I had seen was dressed in a monk's robe, although his face was completely hidden by the hood of his garment. I imagined the person I saw as much taller, more slender and I presumed he had a head full of hair. On the other hand, the person I was looking at, in front of my bed, was short, on the stout side and bald, except for a little hair on both sides of the head. He assured me again that he was who he said he was.

"So why are you appearing to me? Is there a message in all this?"

"Yes! Of course! I wanted to encourage you to read the books I wrote while I was still on earth. At one point, I was going through the very same struggles and doubts that you are experiencing now and I am sure they can be of help to you." Once his message was given, he vanished instantly.

I was stunned, excited...but very curious! Was that *really* the famous author I had read about? Or was I *imagining* the whole thing? Without any doubt, I knew that I was *wide awake* during the whole incident. *Of that I was certain*! I even sat up and walked around for a while, trying to gather my thoughts on the full impact of having actually been visited by someone who had died approximately eight years before. I could not get back to sleep. The clock showed several minutes past 4:00 a.m.

The next morning, I began celebrating Mass with an

emotional excitement that was obvious to the usual forty or so parishioners in attendance. I ignored the homily I had prepared and started talking about the *guest* from the next life, who visited me the night before. My listeners were especially attentive, since I broke from the usual pattern of delivering a brief homily on the Scripture Readings of the day. That was a rare moment for all of us! When I finished relating my story, I decided to risk asking them a delicate question. I inquired whether any of those present had ever experienced a visitation from their loved ones who had passed on or by any other person from the world of spirit. The result was far beyond my expectations! About thirty-five out of forty hands went up. Most of those present were seniors and had lost a spouse...or, at least, someone they loved very much.

We could have stayed there all morning and listened to many beautiful stories based on their personal experiences, but I only allowed a few of them, because of a very full schedule that day.

I will never forget the story a lovely, elderly lady shared with us. Her husband had died about a month before he appeared to her. He told her he received permission to speak to her on a matter of great importance. He told her he had made out a large Insurance Policy recently with *her* as the sole beneficiary. However, he was going to surprise her...and he died quite suddenly without warning! He told her to go down into the basement and go to his workroom. There, she would see a bookcase on the left, with a couple of large books on the second shelf. In one of them, she would find the Insurance Policy. He named the book. Afterwards, he immediately disappeared.

The wife was not accustomed to go into his *private office* where he took care of his financial business and investments. Even since his passing, she had not yet taken anything out of his basement office. Nevertheless, she followed his instructions perfectly and found the Insurance Policy precisely where he indicated. She was grateful for the unexpected and huge financial security he left her!

Surely, it was a vivid testimony of life after death and the closeness that continues with those we love. Thirty-five out of forty is quite a phenomenal percentage of those believing they have communicated in some way with people who have died. I would never have guessed the percentage to be that high. I am speaking of ordinary people who have lost their loved ones.

Considering the experience of so many others, I was becoming convinced I *really was* visited during the night by a well-known writer and Trappist monk. I was going downtown the very next morning; I decided to stop in the Catholic Bookstore located in the same building as the Archdiocesan Offices—on Washington Boulevard in the heart of Detroit. In the bookstore, one of the Religious Sisters in charge asked if she could help me.

I inquired, "Do you have any books by Thomas Merton?"

"Why, yes! Which one are you interested in?"

"All of them," I answered, to her surprise!

She returned with eleven books. I was delighted! *What I really had in mind was hoping to see a picture of my spiritual visitor in one of them.*

I had to know! What did he look like?

Obviously, some of the books were *by* him and some were *about* him. My eyes immediately jumped to the Pictorial Biography of Thomas Merton. I became very excited, paging quickly through the book to see an actual picture of him. There were several!

Yes, indeed! It was the very same person I saw standing in front of my bed the night before! After my initial shock, I turned to Sister who was standing there watching, and said, "I'll take them all!"

"You want *all* eleven books?"

"Yes, I do."

"You must be a great fan of Merton."

"Actually, I really am not, but I believe I am going to be."

All of Merton's books were very interesting, but there was one book that has become my favorite. I have read it three times already and I shall continue to read it. It was just what I needed. My meditations were good, but, as with every good thing, they began to lose some of the excitement and inspiration that I experienced six years prior to 1976. I actually felt as if something were missing, and I believe it affected my whole life, including my Ministry. The book is called the "New Seeds of Contemplation." I highly recommend it to anyone who is serious about meditating.

I still question my experiences. It is difficult enough for me to believe in private revelation from God. It is even more incredible to accept an extraordinary communication with someone who died. I have questioned my own experience over and over. I am totally shocked to receive such an invitation...yet it was an answer to my prayer—one that helped me to stay on the spiritual path I had chosen. Before long, I began to question my doubts: Do we not pray with the expectation that our prayers will be answered...in some way? Is the barrier between this life and the afterlife so fixed that God does not allow life on one level to communicate with another level? After all, from God's point of view, there is no separation. All is one! There is only *One Reality.* We happen to see only a portion of a much larger picture...a very myopic view, I might add.

Traditionally, the Church has always believed in the Communion of Saints and that we all make up the Body of Christ! We are most certainly *connected to each other in Christ.* Help is always given through the Power of God. However, it seems that God has set up a system, in which help may be given directly by Himself or through one of His helpers. We are all familiar with the story about the man who died in a flood and appeared at the Pearly Gates. He complained that God had let him down by not saving him. The water level kept rising and he kept climbing toward the top of his house. Three different times boats were there to take him to safety, which he did not take. Each time he yelled back, "No thanks! God will save me!"

Finally, he drowned! When he complained at the Gates of Heaven that God had let him down, God replied: "Three times I sent you help and you did not take it."

We cannot demand that the Infinite and Supreme Being has to step down to our level every time we want help. The Law of Subsidiarity is apparently a Cosmic Law, as well. It simply means that a problem is resolved at the lowest level. In a factory situation, if something goes wrong, you don't go to the CEO for help, you talk to the foreman or Union steward. If the problem cannot be resolved there, then you go to his superior. If it is still not taken care of, you go to the next one in command. And so on. God seems to follow that pattern...but not always. Jesus, Moses, the Prophets and many Saints were given direct, Divine Guidance according to the Bible and Church History, but that was God's choice. The Mother of Jesus, however, was visited by an angel. Was that any less authentic? Many ordinary and extraordinary people have recorded that they have been helped by angels or saints. We simply *cannot* dictate to God how help should be given. Our role is to recognize the Hand of God and our life's purpose in the blessings we receive. Discernment and prayer form the basis of true assistance from God.

10. YOUR GOD IS TOO SMALL

Each person sits in the prison
of his or her own ideas.
—Albert Einstein

There are many reasons for making such a statement about God being too small. When we were children, religion was taught to us *as children.* Parents were usually the first persons who mentioned the word *God* to us. They used simple language to convey a most immeasurable truth. No arguments were given to prove anything; what we were told was simply an accepted part of life. The young ones, taken to church on weekends, listened to an adult sermon with the mind and understanding of a child. If they attended a parochial school or went to Religious Education classes presented to public school children, the teachers also had to tailor down the immense attributes of an Infinite God so that young children—and they were only children—could perceive, in their little minds, a morsel of the truth about God's existence. Children may have little understanding of who or what God is, but they do have a strong faith. *What they were taught, they believed,* and Jesus compliments children greatly, when He says that unless we become as a little child, we cannot enter into the Kingdom of God. The simple faith of a child is commendable. Yet the Belief

System, in which we place our faith, must go through varying stages of life as we grow up and mature. Consequently, a mature adult is expected to have a mature faith.

Unfortunately, there are many adults today, who still adhere to beliefs that were simplified for their age level as children. As they approached adulthood, many had not *continued to foster and nourish* that faith. Sadly, they neglected the most important relationship in their whole life...the one with their Divine Parent. No wonder so many adult Christians have given up on a god that appears to be for children—a god too limited and too small for modern life.

On the other hand, the average adult today will probably laugh at some of the obsolete and watered-down theology presented to them in their childhood. I meet such people all the time. I remember, years ago, the shock and horrified look on the face of one of the adults updating her childhood beliefs in the RCIA (Rite of Christian Initiation of Adults) Program. A question was asked whether we should let the host (Communion wafer) dissolve in the mouth or chew it. I said I would probably *choke,* if I did not *chew* the large hosts that priests consumed. I explained that you can do either: chew it or let it dissolve. The adult, mentioned above, said that one of her teachers told the children before their First Communion never to bite into the host or chew it—after all, Jesus is somehow present. I stated that the teacher most likely was trying to teach children to distinguish between biting into a baloney sandwich and consuming the Sacred Bread of Christ's Presence. The stage play, "Do Patent Leather Shoes Really Reflect Up?" is filled with obsolete policies that sank into oblivion. Thank God for the Vatican II Council!

I know some good Christian people who still see God as a punisher—or as a divine policeman who never sleeps. That same *god* is not one to love, but rather one to fear! They also believe that same god put a price on our head as if we were common criminals! We were so bad that Jesus had to pay the ransom for our freedom...which cost Him His life. *Something is wrong with this picture!* It makes God the Father look like a tyrant, an unreasonable dictator...the bad guy! Adding to a further distortion of the same analogy, some Christians in recent times, believe that Jesus is ready to exact the same punishment on us as the Father, but His hand is held back by Mary, His Mother. To fear God is to believe that we are separate from God. That is contrary to all of my experiences. We are all *united* to the Source of Life, and it can never be otherwise. We are *loved* one hundred percent by God—and that never changes!

A proper question at this time would be: Aren't we ever punished for having sinned? The answer, of course, is *yes*! However, we are not punished *for* our sins, but rather *by* them. The Lord God of the Universe is not up there slinging punishments at people every time our behavior is less than perfect! God's Love is constant and Perfect. Yet, God being *Perfect*, is not a *perfectionist*! He allows us to make mistakes/sins, as we come to a greater and higher awareness through our experiences...and God is much more patient than we are. *Thank God for that!* Besides, God understands our weaknesses, the misguided thoughts we receive from our culture or upbringing, the genes we inherited, the occasions that lead us astray and much more about us. That is why we are told not to judge. We never see the whole picture of a person who sins privately or whose offense is exposed publicly in the media. Nevertheless, we may be punished *by* our sins/faults/weaknesses. If a man gets drunk, falls down the stairs and breaks a leg, he cannot blame God for that unfortunate outcome. It was his own undoing! He is punished *by* his own mistake! People eating fatty foods, fried foods and an abundance of sweets, cannot say God is punishing them by giving them poor health or a heart attack. *By* their own actions, they are causing such conditions to occur.

One day while I was teaching the Silva Method to about fifty people, I was surprised when a young lady jumped up out of her seat, literally yelling at me. She was upset when I was explaining how we sometimes cause our own death...and God has nothing to do with it.

"Do you mean to tell me that my father *wanted* to die and

leave us? How *dare* you make such an accusation? I loved my dad, and he loved me. That is not possible!"

I replied: "I am not implying that he *deliberately* did any such thing. Of course not! I am sure he loved you all very much."

Then I proceeded to ask her some questions.

"Did your father watch the foods he ate?"

"No. He was terribly over-weight and often ate the wrong foods," was her reply.

"Did he smoke at all?"

"That's another thing. He smoked two packs a day and we warned him often to cut down or stop. It didn't do any good!"

"Did your father drink a lot?"

She gave the same answer. "That was always a problem."

I know that the above conversation sounds unreal, but that is precisely what took place in the class. I ended up by saying, "I rest my case!" She realized very clearly that her father was not trying to commit suicide, but, in reality, he offended his health so badly that it could be called a slow, drawn-out suicide. I use the word *suicide* loosely, yet, his own actions, to all appearances, either caused or contributed to his death. Even if they only *contributed* to his passing, it was still not God wantonly zapping him off the earth.

Sometimes, we are punished for an offense against the law. An embezzler gets caught and ends up in prison. Convicted murderers may spend the rest of their lives behind bars. God is not punishing them. Their own actions are.

In an effort to avoid responsibility, some folks wish to blame the Devil for all their misfortunes. That is not a new concept. Adam blamed Eve and Eve blamed the serpent (Devil) for their disobedience in the Garden of Eden.

The concept of an evil influence in the form of the Devil or Satan in the Bible is a common theme. However, the Biblical image of Satan is not always the one you expect! In the Book of Job, God, the sons of God and Satan were having a discussion. Satan is not described as evil monster from hell, but simply as the *Tester*, the *Challenger*.

Here is the text found in Job 1:6-12.

One day, when the sons of God came to present themselves before the Lord, Satan also came among them. And the Lord said to Satan, "Whence do you come?" Then Satan answered the Lord and said, "From roaming the earth and patrolling it." And the Lord said to Satan, "Have you noticed my servant Job, and that there is no one on earth like him, blameless and upright, fearing God and avoiding evil?" But Satan answered the Lord and said, "Is it for nothing that Job is God-fearing? Have you not surrounded him and his family and all that he has with your protection?

You have blessed the work of his hands, and his livestock are spread over the land. But now put forth your hand and touch anything that he has, and surely he will blaspheme you to your face." And the Lord said to Satan, "Behold, all that he has is in your power; only do not lay a hand upon his person." So Satan went forth from the presence of the Lord.

It is quite obvious that Satan is not displayed here as the Evil One, but rather as one sent by God to test a man who was known for his piety and faithfulness to the Lord. *This they did by agreement!* Actually, in the story, Satan caused the loss of all his possessions, including his family and his cattle. Job remains faithful to the end in spite of his great loss, and the Lord rewards him many times over. It seems that the concept of the Devil or Satan was still going through various stages of development.

In the New Testament, Jesus calls Peter *Satan* when Peter tries to convince Jesus not to go to Jerusalem to fulfill His Messianic Mission. Interfering with God's Plan causes Jesus to exclaim to Peter, "Get behind me, Satan!"

The concept of Satan has been portrayed in many ways through the centuries. Some artists place Satan in charge of the fires of hell, dressed up in a red suit with horns and a pitchfork. Highly imaginative, but adults usually laugh at such an image.

And rightly so! The Scriptures do speak of Lucifer, a fallen angel, along with other angels who fell from God's grace. It would be difficult to identify Lucifer with the Satan of the Job story or with St. Peter who was called "Satan."

Somehow this subject has to be studied further. There is still a tendency to blame Satan for all our woes, just as Adam and Eve did. What is the truth of it all? I am not sure, but surveying the behavior of humanity, it appears that we do not need a Satan to misguide us. We do a good job on our own.

At any rate, blaming God or the Devil for our problems is a far cry from what is expected of a mature perception of God. I borrowed the title, "Your God is Too Small," from J.B. Phillips. That title also represents my views, after more than forty years of observing how people, in general, perceive God as a *concept* rather than a *Live, Active Being* with Whom we interact. Like the old Zen Proverb says: "Do not mistake the finger pointing at the moon, for the moon." In a similar way, just talking about God does not mean we have established a relationship with God!

We live in a Christian country. A good percentage attend church every weekend and follow the understanding of God as predicated by their particular religion. They are considered persons of average intelligence and maturity. I also happen to have many acquaintances who are among the *unchurched*, equally intelligent and mature. The unchurched simply do not see how the God of a formal, organized religion can account for life in a modern world. Moving further, they question how a God, limited to a particular religion and encased in a particular church, could be big enough to create and comprehend the most sophisticated, high-tech, scientific knowledge ever known on this planet—deserving the highest admiration and respect. The god that many adults believe in, is much too small to operate this tiny, little planet...not to mention the operation of a whole universe. They think he can't even hear the complaints of so many people shouting, "Why doesn't God do something about this?" Their perception of such a god is no God! Those complaining also need to reflect on what they are saying.

The major reason why the world is in such a mess is because, as co-creators with God, there are millions and millions of self-centered, instead of God-centered, negative-thinking people who are sending out dangerous thoughts of hate and destruction. Each one of these hate thoughts is a powerful energy which, when multiplied by millions, makes a drastic puncture in the fragile fabric of world peace. When peace of mind is gone, fear and anger, anxiety and violence are only too happy to permeate our world. We can't blame God for what we ourselves are causing...and without regard!

When it comes to conscience, God may be seen, unfortunately by many, as a policeman on perpetual duty. Although every person is given a conscience which distinguishes right from wrong, nevertheless, conscience can become customized, fettered, narrowed or even distorted by our upbringing, training and propaganda. Children are great imitators. Obviously, whatever language the parents speak on this planet, regardless of which country, children will speak the same tongue with the same accent and idioms, including the moral values, taboos and superstitions of the parents. The god of the parents becomes the god of their children.

There are still some folks pleading with God to help them win the lotto. That request is much larger than the questioner realizes. Their concern is to get big bucks! And God *can* do it, because God can do anything! Yes, God can, but the Almighty Lord of the Universe is not to be reduced to a mere fortune-teller to help someone get rich quick! Yet, there are multi-millions who desire to win the big one and someone *is* destined to win. To answer why a particular person, out of so many, is destined to win—I say *destined*, because there are no accidents—you would have to know all the factors involved in each person's spiritual path...which only God knows!

Another god passed on from parent to child is the image of an old man in a long, white beard and a kind smile. He sits on the throne in heaven, and being old, is old-fashioned. In fact, in our lifetime, a mixed group of older adolescents were asked to answer without hesitation or reflection, "Do you think God understands radar?" Nearly every person replied "No!" *What would an old man know about nuclear physics, quantum mechanics or thermodynamics?*

When we were children, we used to say, "My dad is better than your dad!" A verbal battle would ensue. As adults, discussing and comparing religions, there is a tendency to make the same comment with the same analogy, but different words: "My religion is better than your religion!" Such statements reduce God to a minor god, who is jealous, has an ego problem and is not fully developed yet.

To an outsider, who has no particular affiliation with any formal religion, it is understandable that there are many different denominations, each with a different set of beliefs. What may be difficult to comprehend is how each one insists on having the exclusive claim to be the *right one*. Jesus Himself answered their claims when He said, "By their fruits, you will know them." Of course, if any denomination can prove that the entire membership of their particular religion are *perfect Christians* worldwide, some credibility might be given it. I suspect that all religious denominations have *some* saintly members, outstanding in virtue, and famous for their integrity and holiness. *No religion is composed of perfect Saints,* according to my knowledge! The Catholic Faith has produced many canonized Saints throughout it's two-thousand year history. There are outstanding Catholics living today, but that percentage is small! In an act of honesty, the Catholic Church condemned a policy that was prevalent in my younger years that boldly affirmed, "Outside the Catholic Church, there is no salvation." Fr. Feeney, a Catholic priest, who promoted it strongly, was eventually excommunicated for heresy. Catholics believe that the Church goes back to the time of Christ in an unbroken line of faith. However, the Church is not deaf to the rest of the world. You can't put God in a box! "The Spirit blows where it wills," Jesus reminds us.

To one who is not Christian, the thought must occur why the Christian Churches do not unite and become one! Christ, obviously, is the foundation stone of every Church established in His Name. Logic would say that it is a complicated affair, with each Church holding to its differences with sincerity and confidence. Could it be that each Christian Church believes—consciously, or perhaps unconsciously—that God may actually be Lutheran, Methodist, Catholic, Presbyterian, Episcopalian, Baptist or whatever? Does not each denomination need to remove itself from an inadequate, little god and realize the Grandeur and Immensity of the one True God? How can God, Who is Infinite, be classified, contained or boxed in by finite creatures on a tiny little planet in this incredibly vast Universe? Almighty God is much too big!

The discoveries of modern science, astronomy, psychology, parapsychology, quantum mechanics, higher mathematics, etc. have profoundly changed the *size* of the Creator in the eyes of a thinking person today. If there is an Infinite Mind behind the cosmic and extraterrestrial complexities of the phenomena that earthlings can observe, then it is that of a Being tremendous in Power and Wisdom: it is emphatically not that of a little god. J.B. Phillips maintains that:

Many men and women today are living, often with inner dissatisfaction...not because they are particularly wicked or selfish or, as the old-fashioned would say , godless, but because they have not found, with their adult minds, a God big enough to account for life, big enough to fit in with the new scientific age, big enough to command their highest admiration and respect.

However, as an unknown author put it: "The sort of thing which outrages reason and sets sanity rocking on her seat is to be told that *Almighty God* can only operate through one particular belief system." Can the *Creator* be so small or are the *minds* that invent such a god so small? I love Einstein's view of the many different religions on this planet. Symbolically, he sees a large wagon wheel in the sky, with each religion as a spoke pointing to the center of the wheel—where God is—yet, each religion believes it is the only one following the true path to God.

So, just how big is the real God? A lot bigger than anyone can imagine! All Theologians, Bible scholars, scientists, philosophers, poets—together could never fathom even the tiniest percentage of God's greatness. God, in the strictest sense, cannot be classified, described adequately, defined, explained, diagnosed, etc., even with all the superlatives in the dictionary, because our *descriptions*, being limited, merely limit the Infinite. We have no idea of what Infinite means. We have only finite minds to work with. That is not to say, we don't occasionally get a *glimpse of God or a momentary experience of God,* but to convey this experience to another lacks the vocabulary in English or in any language. Similarly, how can the parameters of a single drop of water adequately describe the entire ocean?

Jesus speaks of God as Father. That is the relationship He establishes with God. We can do that, too! A philosopher, on the other hand, will see God as The First Cause! Not surprisingly, Plato, Socrates and Aristotle viewed God as The First principle. Although we may not *understand* God, we can certainly form a *bond* or *relationship* with our Creator. God is truly a *Divine, Cosmic Lover,* and the greatest romance in the Universe is how this Infinite Being can love you or me as we are, with our faults, our ignorance, our limitations and our false beliefs. This is a *love story* that re-sounds throughout the Universe! It is your story...and will always be!

11. PRAYER IS A RELATIONSHIP

Prayer does not change God,
but changes the one who prays.
                    —Soren Kierkegaard

One person with God
is always in the majority.
                    —John Knox

Prayer takes on many forms since each of us pray uniquely when we address God directly. There are established vocal prayers which people say when they are in a group setting, which, of course, are necessary. Otherwise Community Prayers would be impossible.

What is most important in any prayer, is the *intention* one has in mind. If the prayer is nothing more than a preponderance of words, repeated over and over, and thrown in God's direction, I am sure they would be quite meaningless. Just saying or repeating a lot of words is not convincing, neither to the one praying nor to the one listening. *What is convincing* is a truly heartfelt prayer from the depths of one's soul—a sincere communication with our Creator! That prayer is always heard and always granted...well, granted according to what is best for us in the Mind of God.

What does the Master Jesus say about prayer? His comment is very challenging! Most of our prayers are not with the attitude He recommends. Consider these words, comparing the advice Jesus gives, with your method of prayer. He said:

> Have faith in God. I tell you solemnly, if you say to this mountain, "Get up and throw yourself into the sea," with no hesitation in your heart, but believing that what you say will happen, it will be done for you. I tell you therefore, everything you ask and pray for, believe that you have it already, and it will be yours. And when you stand in prayer, forgive whatever you have against anybody, so that God, your Father in heaven, may forgive your failings, too. (Mark 11: 22-25)

First of all, how many people do you know pray with such confidence—that nothing is impossible for God? If that were not true, which God or gods are we talking about? Let's take another look at Jesus' recommended disposition for prayer: *Have faith in God.* If one's faith is weak, so is the prayer. If one's faith is unsure, negative or doubtful, so is the prayer.

I believe that when Jesus said that you could move a

mountain and command it to throw itself into the sea, He was serious! There are no limits with God! All things are possible. The essential requirement is *"believing that what he says will happen..."* The belief is supported and strengthened by having *"...no hesitation in his heart..."* The Lord Jesus is not talking about games one could play. On the contrary, if there were a truly serious reason to move a mountain, it would happen if there were no hesitation or doubt in the mind of the person praying.

There are two more items of supreme importance. This one is probably the hardest of all: *"Believe that you have it already, and it will be yours."* This is a difficult request for the human mind. We are living in *time*. To say that we have already received something that our senses indicate is not ours yet, seems contrary to reason. It *would be* contrary to reason if the only reality were this three-dimensional, physically-limited world in which we live and nothing else.

The incredible truth is that what we are experiencing here is only a tiny portion of a much larger picture, without knowing how the process of being co-creator with God actually works.

In God's World—beyond time and space—what we ask for may be accomplished immediately. Every prayer is heard and every prayer is answered. However, the answer is not always manifested physically in our lives. Sometimes, there is an immediate result, such as a healing of an incurable disease.

Other times, the healing in our physical world is accomplished slowly, almost in segments of time. Regardless, the difference between what we *want* and what we *need* remains the issue. Understanding and attunement with the Creative Forces of God and spiritual healing, as the primary objective in prayers of petition, changes our whole perspective.

Prayer, of course, is not only a matter of asking and receiving. There is much more to prayer than that! Prayer is about *relationship*! One of the major reasons for praying is to establish and maintain a strong relationship with God. Prayer may be described as a conversation with Someone we love and with Whom we want to stay very close. In a word, prayer is communication with our Heavenly Father and Best Friend.

In Psalm 84:2, David longs for a close relationship with God: "My heart and my flesh cry out for the Living God!" It works both ways: We draw near to God, and God, in turn, draws near to us, as we are reminded by St. James in his fourth chapter.

Many people are faithful to their prayers every day. There are countless people of every faith throughout the world who pray as if it were a ritual. They have *set-prayers* that are easy to say in the Presence of the Almighty One. The *rosary* of Catholic Christians, the *prayer beads* of the Buddhist, the repeated incantation of the Hindu *mantra*, special prayers recited five times a day by faithful Moslems, the daily ritual of the Jewish

Kaddish, recited in the synagogue or at the death of a close relative—all of these are very impressive. People praying daily to the Creator revives my hope in humanity.

Many Christians recite the Lord's Prayer or Psalm 23 (the Good Shepherd Psalm) when alone. For years, Catholic Christians have been offering up the Rosary with the greatest devotion they could summon from the depths of their soul. Priests recite their Breviary which is called the Divine Office or the official prayers of the church.

There are many more ways to communicate with God. All, of course, are valid and may be heart-felt, soul-stirring or even rapturous. God may be called by different names, but there is only *one God.* God may be known as Allah, Adonai, Tao, Brahma, Great Spirit or a host of other names. The *name* given to God is not as important as the *relationship* with God.

Prayers are powerful when combined. Every church, synagogue or mosque is virtually a *power house* of prayer. God speaks every language and every dialect and is familiar with every accent, drawl, brogue, sign language or whatever type of communication of which humans are capable.

Unfortunately, some folks only pray when they are with a Faith Community in a church setting. At home, there is not much attention given to the constant and abiding Presence of God. Upon awakening and starting a new day, there is often not even a mention of gratitude for another day and another opportunity to serve God and others. Sometimes people even forget to ask for a blessing or say a prayer of thanks before meals, ignoring the fact that food is a gift from Mother Nature, the Hand of God upon the earth. Particularly, at night before retiring, is it not appropriate to be grateful for another day and also to petition for Divine protection during the night, when we enter the unconscious state?

I have only mentioned the *basics* of prayer directed to the Creator, who sustains our life every moment of every day. I certainly recommend moving to a higher level of communication. By that, I mean talking to God in our own words. Fixed prayers written by someone else are *good*. But a spontaneous expression from the heart is far more *authentic*. When talking to a friend, would you recite some words that are obviously memorized and even out of place? Would your friend not look at you and wonder what on earth you are talking about? She may be puzzled by why you are not talking to her. She may even worry about you, thinking you are on some ego-trip, showing how well you can memorize some beautiful words from Literature or Poetry—or even a quote from Sacred Scripture. Naturally, a conversation would be impossible under such conditions.

I am not trying to degrade official prayers which one says before God in private prayer. A rosary, for example, can be a wonderful exchange with God through the guided imagery of the different *mysteries* or events in the life of Christ or His Mother. A person can enter a very deep level of meditation while repeating words that are fixed and exact. My point is that the repetition of words alone is not prayer. The *intention*, plus the *effort*, to turn the prayers into a channel of communication with God is everything! A quoted prayer that one has *internalized* may be a very sincere and powerful prayer.

At some point, however, in praying to God, would it be demanding too much to say a few words about a situation that has come up, expressing some concern about the conditions at work or at home, addressing the Almighty about your fears and anxieties? Would it not be an appropriate time to offer prayers for a sick family member or a friend, or to say simply, *I love you*, or, perhaps, to discuss how things got better or worse since the last time you spoke to your Creator/ Father/Mother/Best Friend?

Our communication with God says a lot about who we are and who God is. Our self-image has a lot to do with our relationship to God. The experience of a relationship with God differs for each one of us, as does everything else. If we feel loved and accepted by God, there is no power on this earth which can destroy such a happy and healthy self image. "If you, O Lord, are for us, who can be against us?"

If we feel distant from God, there will be very little communication with that Someone who seems to be so far away. At the same time, every relationship we have with ourselves, our family, our friends and co-workers will be tempered by and filtered by our relationship with our Divine Parent. I repeat, that our relationship with God is the *basic, cosmic, and universal bond* we establish with the Source of all Reality. All other apparent realities and actual relationships *hinge* on the nature of this bond with Divinity. We are never the same after praying sincerely. True prayer is always followed up by some kind of action. We can never be the same once we have an ongoing and lively relationship with God. Something has to happen! We may think a little differently, viewing reality from a different perspective and recognizing others as siblings of the same Divine Parent. Again, because of the sense of *oneness*, we very possibly may respond to others' needs as if they were our own, remembering the earth as a global village watched over carefully by Divine Providence. These are only some of the natural results, following genuine prayer. We continue to move endlessly forward and upward as Teilhard de Chardin would say.

St. Paul is an excellent example of how an encounter with the Lord changes one's life forever. The action was first taken by Christ. Paul responded with all his heart and was totally transformed! He became a great disciple of Christ, and championed the cause of Christianity wherever he went. He needed to talk to God frequently because he was almost nonstop in trouble with his former colleagues and challenged firmly by brilliant thinkers among the gentile nations. The opposition to St. Paul was not just verbal. He was imprisoned, tortured, publicly rejected, forced out of town and beaten...but he never lost hope. He prayed often and received faithful Guidance from above. Even when shipwrecked, and urged by the Holy Spirit to take long trips to foreign countries amid great hardship, he never faltered because of his extraordinary relationship with God. Of course, God gave him miraculous gifts to accompany him on his many travels. His gifts he used wisely and became one of the most well-known Saints and one of the greatest missionaries of all time.

We may not get knocked off a horse or beaten over the head to get our attention, but God is never far away and takes us by the hand when we are ready. Paul must have been ready, even though he persecuted Christians and had them imprisoned. He did it out of a sincere conviction that Christians were victims of false belief and also dangerous enemies. Christ simply channeled Paul's energies, changing him into a defender of Christians.

Joan of Arc had a similar problem. As a young girl she believed her relationship to God was very real and personal. She claimed that God sent her spiritual guides who advised her in making some decisions for herself and for the Dauphin who was the prince and heir to the throne of France.

According to Alban Butler's Lives of the Saints, Joan of Arc led a very eventful life with Divine Guidance:

Joan of Arc was born on the feast of the Epiphany 1412, at Domremy, a little village of Champagne on the bank of the Meuse. Her father, Jacques d'Arc, was a peasant farmer of some local standing, a worthy man, frugal and rather morose; but his wife was a gentle affectionate mother to their five children. Joan was very young when Henry V of England invaded France, overran Normandy and claimed the crown of the insane king, Charles VI. France, in the throes of civil war, between the contending parties of the Duke of Burgundy and Orleans, was in no condition to put up an adequate resistance. St. Joan was in her fourteenth year when she experienced the earliest of those supernatural manifestations, which were to lead her through the path of patriotism to death at the stake. At first, it was a single voice addressing her apparently from near by, and accompanied by a blaze of light: afterwards, as the voices increased in number, she was able to see her spiritual guides whom she identified as St. Michael, St. Catherine, St. Margaret and others. Only very gradually did they unfold her mission.

Her Voices gave her no rest even when she protested that she was a poor girl who could neither ride nor fight. They replied that is was God's Will! She then consented to follow their guidance. Joan correctly predicted a serious defeat of the French and gained recognition. She became the *Maid of Orleans*, a legendary and great leader who would free the French from English occupation. She was introduced to Prince Charles who had purposely disguised himself but she identified him at once and, by a secret sign communicated to her by her Voices and imparted by her to him alone, she obliged him to believe in the supernatural nature of her mission. Having gained his confidence, she then asked him for soldiers whom she might lead to the relief of Orleans. By May 8, the English forts which surrounded Orleans had been captured and the siege raised after she herself had been wounded in the breast by an arrow. Having recovered, Joan of Arc as the Maid of Orleans, was allowed to undertake a short campaign on the Loire with the Duc d'Alenqon, one of her best friends. It was completely successful and ended with a victory at Patay in which the English forces under Sir John Fastolf suffered a crushing defeat.

On July 17, 1429, Charles VII was solemnly crowned, Joan standing at his side with her standard. That event, which completed the mission originally entrusted to her by her Voices, marked also the close of her military successes. She was captured in another battle and sold to the English, who wanted desperately to dispose of her life. They falsely condemned her as a sorceress and a heretic. She was burned at the stake, never losing her intimate relationship with Almighty God. She was only twenty-three years old. Later, her family appealed for a reopening of the case. Pope Callistus III appointed a commission for this purpose. On July 7, 1456, they reversed the false trial and verdict. She was completely justified and exonerated. She was canonized a Saint on May 16, 1920. Her relationship with God and with her spirit guides sent by God, gave her the strength and faith she needed to face a most painful death.

I repeat: our relationship with God is everything! It is not always convenient for the average parent to get away from the family for a few days in order to make a retreat. Yet, it is of tantamount importance to spend time in prayer, reading the Sacred Scriptures, and reinforce our relationship with our Divine Parent. Of all the ways possible to deepen our bond with God, *solitude* offers the most opportune moments for such an encounter. The hustle and bustle, the distracting noise level and all the while keeping the pot boiling on the stove is not the best atmosphere for bonding with the Invisible Lord. That is not to say that we are unable to communicate or even unite deeply with God, even under the above and worse circumstances. God is always available and at every moment. Nevertheless, statistics would show that a very busy atmosphere is not as conducive to fostering a deep relationship with God. For this reason, priests are strongly urged to make a private retreat at least once a year. Maybe I need more help than the average person, but I usually make *two retreats* each year. If I had time, I would make that three!

The goal, of course, is to raise one's awareness to the degree that everything is a prayer: work in an office or a factory, cleaning house or washing dishes, caring for young children, cooking, mowing the lawn—it really doesn't matter—all actions can nourish us spiritually as God's family. With the proper intention, the result would be *a life of prayer.* Through the example of highly evolved beings, demonstrated in the lives of the saints and great spiritual leaders, the common thread they shared was the continual and unending sense of oneness with God or the Great Spirit. Another outstanding benefit of being united with our Source is the sense of wholeness or holiness. That can only happen when creature and Creator are one.

While we are in this three-dimensional world, we are overwhelmed by the incredible signs of growth everywhere. We get surprised every year in the Spring when we are surrounded by new life, as the trees come alive again, and bushes and flowers are filled with color and surprise. Growth is a natural phenomenon and it will always remain an exciting part of life.

We don't question it; we don't challenge it; we simply presume that Mother Nature (or God's action in the world) provides us with beautiful surroundings each year, as we experience the change of seasons.

Somehow, we fail to realize that the same Source of growth all around us expects *us* to grow as well. The growth of our bodies is obvious, of course! But we are not as fully conscious of the necessity for spiritual growth. It takes a few years of growing up and maturing to see that spiritual progress or spiritual growth is absolutely the most important quest we face in life. Not just in Springtime, but all year long. Connected to that concept is the relationship we establish with our Creator, with others and with our environment. In fact, it takes a lifetime to realize that we are not owners, but rather stewards of all that we have and because we are created in the image and likeness of *God—we have to keep reminding* ourselves—we are co-creators with God.

Developing a deep relationship with God joins heaven to earth...not just when we die, but *now*! The spiritual growth of our life with God is the greatest reality. And yet it is unseen.

It is only with the heart that one can see rightly;
what is essential is invisible to the eye.

That is what the fox said to the prince in Antoine de Saint-

143

Exupery's book *The Little Prince*, but that which is invisible is not out of reach to our soul. This apparent world of separation deceives us if we do not get past the illusion of what is real and what is unreal. Prayer is the key to a clearer recognition of reality. Again, prayer is definitely not a form of *escape* from reality, but rather, an *encounter* with reality.

All through life we are face with the never-ending quest of seeking the eternal realities: Who is God? What is our relationship to God? How do we fit into the Master Plan of Creation...the Universe? What is our purpose in being here? Do we have a goal/mission to accomplish? How do we find out the answers to these and other unending questions which frequently cross our minds? Only from within are we able to evaluate what is spiritually worthwhile, as we journey through life. Without an active prayer-life, we could deteriorate into materialism, which is not satisfying to the human spirit. Even worse, life would seem hopeless!

Through the years, I have met a surprising number of people who give little thought to a life of prayer—and establishing a relationship with God. Most people I know, on the other hand, do pray in their own way—maybe a short prayer to God for their families, a word of thanks, a petition for a member of the family in the hospital. They keep in contact with God. Those, however, who have lost contact with the Creator, seem to be satisfied with current thought and values in the world. They are just drifting and they seriously wonder what is missing in their lives. Of course, it would be the lack of internal or spiritual growth. There is an expression in Spanish which describes such a person: "El camarón que se duerme, se lo lleva la corriente." Freely translated would be: "the shrimp which is asleep drifts along with the current...that is to say: is going nowhere!" They simply hope that things go well, not knowing that they are co-creators. Others do seek something better, something that will throw light on their lives, giving them understanding and knowledge of a Higher Power that is alive and active.

Defining prayer will fall short of the full impact of its experiences, because it is so personal and yet, so powerful. Everyone has heard the simple definition that "Prayer is talking to God." But there is a much deeper view on this. *Attitude* in prayer is everything, as demonstrated in Jesus' parable:

> Two men went up into the temple to pray, the one a Pharisee, and the other a Publican. The Pharisee stood and prayed thus, "God, I thank thee, that I am not as other men are, extortioners, unjust, adulterers, or even as this Publican. I fast twice a week, I give tithes of all that I possess." And the Publican, standing afar off, would not lift up so much as his eyes unto heaven, but struck his breast, saying, "God, be merciful to me a sinner." I tell you, this man (The

Publican) went down to his house justified rather than the other. *(Luke 18:10-14)*

Also, prayer is not merely what we say to God. It is the process of responding thoughtfully to what God has already said and what the Lord is constantly saying to us through the words of Holy Scripture. For this reason, the Bible and other inspired writings are an important part of our ongoing conversation with God.

One way to develop prayer, or talking to God, is to open the Scriptures to a specific page or at random and reflect on the meaning of the text, with a view to understanding more clearly God's way of relating to us! Knowing what is important to God throws much light on our desire to follow a path that is pleasing to God. Slowly, we become more and more comfortable with the knowledge of Divine Values and more confident to establish a conversation with our Divine Parent. For example, as the father of a family prays in response to the words of I Corinthians 13, he will know God's view about true love and apply it to his relationship with his children. It may be the phrase "love is patient, love is kind," that impresses him about his treatment of the kids after a full day's work. Even when one is tired, there is still the need for a loving and kind treatment of one's family. It would be a welcomed change in attitude and behavior.

Be silent, and listen to God. Let your heart be in such a state of preparation that His Spirit may impress upon you such virtues as will please Him. This silence of all outward and earthly affection and of human thoughts within us is essential if we are to hear this Voice.

It may not be an audible voice. But you will know it's the Voice of the Spirit when you hear the truths of Scripture speaking gently, lovingly and forcefully to the circumstances and concerns of your life.

Listening to God will lead to actions as well as words. Words are just the beginning because our response must go well beyond that. It will give us encouraging words to say to those sick or in hopeless situations. It will give us the fortitude to face our daily problems. It will also give us the strength to finally let go of a sinful attitude or habit.

In other words, prayer and action are wedded to each other and the more profound our prayer-filled relationship to God, the more surprising and radical the action may be. It may lead us to the bedside of a dying friend or find us in line picketing a company for its unfair employment policy. It may send us into our past, in order to deal with some unresolved pain we have either received ourselves or caused another. Our well-planned life, our comfort zone, may be drastically altered. This happens because when we pray to God, we are not praying to a Being who is static, dull, inactive or dormant. We are speaking of the Creator Who is continually creating, making things anew. He is the living God, the Almighty One Who touches our lives with an awesome Power and transforms us with an unpredictable outcome. God has the last word! He may simply leave us just as we are.

When we pray to God, we usually believe that we are the ones taking the action, that we are the ones initiating a conversation with God. In reality, we may simply be responding to God's Grace that urges us to pray. St. Paul speaks of God loving us before we loved Him. That is the meaning given to the words of Jesus in the Book of Revelation: "Behold, I stand at the door and knock." (Rev. 3:20). There is a door without a doorknob and the only way it opens is from the inside. Christ stands at the door of our heart and asks to enter. We then decide to open the door or not. If we do, we may call our response *prayer*!

PART THREE

I have to get a little more technical in this se... ...s unavoidable, considering the implications. Science is not easy to simplify or to offer in clear terms. And yet, it is the other side of Metaphysics, along with religion. My main goal in life has been to pursue truth. There are so many superstitions and false premises adhered to by the educated, as well as the uneducated. Truth is quite elusive in a world filled with conflicting views on almost everything.

The vastness of the Universe, the quest for what is *real* and the beliefs based on observation alone are both confusing and disturbing, to say the least. Where does a person start on a meaningful journey toward the stars? Why must every religion be re-visited and seen in its proper perspective—which is considered *paranormal*? I will explain why I believe this so!

On a spectrum between the most fundamental attitude on one end and the most liberal on the other, how can people living in the same country, the same city, the same neighborhood and being raised in a similar atmosphere be so different from each other?

My reflections center on my own experience and studies. You may or may not agree with me. And that is all right—if we are, at least, listening to what each other has to say.

12. OUR PLACE IN THE UNIVERSE

You are a child of the universe,
no less than the trees and the stars.
You have a right to be here,
and whether or not it is clear to you,
no doubt the Universe is unfolding
as it should.

—Max Ehrmann,

I am neither a professional scientist nor an astronomer. I majored in Philosophy and minored in English when I graduated from Sacred Heart Seminary College in 1952. Nevertheless, since my childhood, long before I entered the Seminary, I have always been interested in the heavens and its possible influence on us. Later, I wondered if there were any scientific explanation for the belief that the stars and the neighboring planets really had an impact on our lives.

There is not a single human being I have ever met, who has not pondered the question of our existence on this planet. As a child, it was delightful to discover the *whys* and *wherefores* of our environment by testing just about everything in sight to see how things work, break so easily or spill so smoothly on the floor...to which parents will unhappily testify.

Typically, as a child, it soon became increasingly clear to me—and the average child—that there were laws that had to be obeyed, such as not playing with *fire* and being careful not to *fall* down the stairs. Then there were biological laws to be met, such as *eating* to survive.

Respect for Mother Nature and the starry heavens grew with the years, especially, when for the first time, I witnessed and marveled at a full moon floating out in space. I realized, at a young age, that there is a power out there that is far beyond anything we are capable of fully understanding or duplicating.

In fact, my mind simply short-circuited when I discovered from books on astronomy that there are billions—perhaps an infinite number—of stars, galaxies, comets, meteors and now, black holes, all through the Universe. More recently, there has been genuine evidence that there may be life elsewhere in space.

It is very easy to limit our life, our thinking, our imagination and our belief system to the parameters of the earth. We often forget that our earth/home is a little point in space, surrounded by billions of other stars and—very possibly—millions of other planets like our own.

The youngsters studying science or astronomy today, probably know more than the great astronomers of centuries ago. It was only in the sixteenth century that Nicholas

Copernicus, a German/Prussian, who is considered the father of modern astronomy, was credited for the theory that the earth revolved on its own axis and also orbited the sun along with the other planets in the Solar System. He began his serious study in 1507.

Later, Galileo Galilei found himself in serious trouble early in the seventeenth century for propounding the Copernican theories concerning the Solar System. He was called to Rome and was forced by the Inquisition to recant his theories. The thought of the day was that the earth was the center of the Universe and everything revolved around it. That proof was based on observation alone.

Although a little late, Galileo's theories were accepted posthumously by Pope John Paul II and forgiveness was sought for the treatment he received at the hands of the Church centuries before. We have come a long way since then. Young students today would consider it unthinkable that the huge sun, a thousand times larger than the earth, would be revolving around a stationary earth.

Since the construction of the famous Mt. Palomar telescope with its 200 inch mirror and the unrivaled Hubble telescope orbiting in space at this moment, the Universe is becoming more and more familiar.

The Universe is filled with galaxies. Before 1900, no one knew what a galaxy was; then, by 1920, a select number of astronomers knew. By 1924, this knowledge was shared by all astronomers. Galaxies are the largest single aggregate of stars in the Universe. They are to astronomy what atoms and sub-atomic particles are to physics. Galaxies are phenomenal, immense and mysterious. As incredible as they are, we happen to live on one. Our Solar System is part of an unbelievably large grouping of stars known as The Milky Way. Our nebula or galaxy, the Milky Way, is composed of more than 100 billion Star Systems. A select number of stars, if not all, may have planets similar to those in our Solar System. As of this writing, scientists have recently discovered about twelve planets orbiting other stars in outer space. These, and other stars, are moving in rhythm with other star systems and galaxies. In fact, all galaxies, quasars, comets and meteors are all moving in what may be described as an enormous Cosmic Dance. The Dance of the smallest atom and the grandiose Dance of the largest galaxy is beautiful to behold!

Our sun is part of the Cosmic Dance, shining brightly every day for us and, in a very real sense, is our life-giver. Without question, we are basically *star people*. The earth and everything on it, including our bodies, originally came from the Sun. It would be true to say that our bodies are crystallized sunlight. The same is true for the trees, mountains and flowers, etc.

Such beauty throughout the Universe is not an accidental, random, unpredictable result out of a *hodge-podge of cosmic primordial soup.* I believe that nothing happens without the guiding Hand of the Creator. Everything appears at its proper moment. The Unlimited Power of God has been, and still is, in control of all Cosmic Forces. It is my firm belief that *the whole Universe is unfolding and everything is on time!*

Here is an excerpt from Pierre Teilhard de Chardin's book *Hymn of the Universe.* He was a Jesuit theologian, scientist, geologist and paleontologist. He sees the whole Universe and all of humanity being prepared precisely for the coming of Christ into this world.

The prodigious expanses of time which preceded the first Christmas were not empty of Christ: they were imbued with the influx of His power. It was the ferment of His conception that stirred up the cosmic masses and directed the initial developments of the biosphere. It was the travail preceding His birth that accelerated the development of instinct and the birth of thought upon the earth. Let us have done with the stupidity which makes a stumbling-block of the endless eras of expectancy imposed on us by the Messiah; the fearful, anonymous labors of primitive man, the beauty fashioned through its age-long history by ancient Egypt, the anxious expectancies of Israel, the patient distilling of the attar of oriental mysticism, the endless refining of wisdom by the Greeks: all these were needed before the Flower could blossom on the rod of Jesse and of all humanity. All these preparatory processes were cosmically and biologically necessary that Christ might set foot upon our human stage. And all this labor was set in motion by the active, creative awakening of His Soul, inasmuch as that Human Soul had been chosen to breathe life into the Universe. When Christ first appeared before men in the arms of Mary, he had already stirred up the world.

In greater detail, it is now an accepted fact that the earth is a global village. There are more books and more newspapers available in the reader's market than ever before in the history of the human race. And yet, there is much more than that! Previous civilizations did not have the advantage of television and the satellite system in outer space, relay systems on the earth, fiber optics, computers, stored gigabytes of information, the Internet and countless extensions of the above.

In the course of time, Mother Nature has revealed many of Her secrets. It is now common knowledge that the tides are affected in rhythm with the moon; that moon cycles and menstrual cycles are related; that the internal biorhythm of every human being follows a pattern from the day we are born: the physical cycle, being twenty-two days, with critical days and peak performance days, on specific best and worst days of each month, for the rest of our life; also, the emotional cycle, consisting of twenty-eight days—again, the best and worse days of the month every two weeks; lastly, there is the intellectual cycle of thirty-three days in which, on specific days, we are mentally alert and sharp...or, on critical days, mentally disoriented. All three rhythms follow a definite pattern and are predictable.   In fact, I read in a book on Biorhythms that Japanese and German pilots are not permitted to fly commercial flights on critical days—insuring the best performance for the sake of security.

Butterflies are an interesting phenomenon. The death of a crawling caterpillar in a cocoon and emerging as a butterfly, through a metamorphosis, is a fact to which we can all witness. It is an incredible sign of new life—visible and observable before our very eyes. Just as mysterious is the lengthy journey of the monarch butterfly, which flies south each year from Minnesota, Illinois or Michigan, for example, and settles in a designated place in Mexico. The sky becomes so cluttered with the many thousands of them that the sun is completely blocked out. The monarch delivers its larvae and the young offspring, in due season, flies back exactly to the location up north where its parent came from—a place it had never been before. And the cycle continues. This is only a small example of the biogenetics that is taking place continually before our very eyes.

More broadly speaking, revelations and discoveries take place or unfold when our global awareness on earth is ready for the next step into Higher Consciousness. Are inventions that raise the awareness of the human race overnight happenings purely by *chance* or *accident?* I doubt it! I really don't believe in accidents—from our point of view...yes, but not from God's point of view! They occur only when the time is right and when humankind is ready to advance on the scale of *awareness or need.* Some of the most practical *inventions* happened, to all appearances, quite by accident. I believe those *accidents* were directed by Divine Guidance and happened only because the timing was right in our development.

For example, there is a microwave oven in practically every home now but not before 1947. An American, Percy Le Baron Spencer, while working on the emission of short-wave electromagnetic energy, discovered the microwave accidentally. In 1946, he was doing research for the Raytheon Company, when he noticed that the microwaves had melted a piece of candy in his pocket. Only then, did he realize the enormous benefit of microwaves in cooking. As we now know, microwaves directly affect the food they cook by creating within the foodstuff a molecular vibration that produces heat. The microwave oven was ready for marketing the following year.

Another *surprise discovery:* Velcro is found in nearly every home today! It often replaces shoe laces on tennis shoes, some metal zippers and often used on children's tote bags and packaging. Velcro is a Swiss discovery that dates from 1948. Returning from a day's hunting, the engineer, Georges de Mestral, often noticed that thistle blossoms clung to his clothing. He became very curious as to the reason for this happening. He was a persistent fellow! So, one day, he placed the thistles under a microscope. He then realized that each of the thistle blossoms contained tiny hooks allowing it to catch onto fabrics. It then occurred to him to fix similar hooks on fabric strips which would cling together and serve as fasteners. Another of Mother Nature's secrets unveiled!

It took about eight years to develop the basic product: two nylon strips, one of which contained thousands of small hooks, and the other, even smaller loops. When the two strips were pressed together, they formed a quick and practical fastener. The invention was named *Velcro* (from two French words: *velour,* meaning velvet and *crochet*, meaning hook.) It was patented worldwide in 1957.

The process of discovery is moving rapidly today due to high-tech methods which accelerate the whole process of generating something new, something more efficient, something that makes life easier and more exciting. So, where are these new things leading us? Do they help us to discover who we are and what we doing on planet Earth? We know we are here...our senses tell us that! How did we get here? Why are we born in *this* world? Where are we going? Is everything mechanical, like clockwork? Do we have a choice in the matter? Is everything by chance? When we were conceived, were we a *random pick* among the possibilities, like a lotto number?

I recall, in my earlier years, many times yelling out to the Universe/God/Anybody out there: *please tell me why I am here!* Even though I had been gifted with an incredible vision with three of my siblings, Rose, Billie and Tony, and witnessed several miraculous healings with my mother in Carey, Ohio, I still needed affirmation, from time to time.

Eventually, I learned a great deal about myself, my purpose, my direction, my temporary goals, and, most importantly, my eternal goal. Scripture helped a lot. I was quite excited the first time I realized that *there was a time for each of us to be born, and a time to die...including major events between them.*

Our birth was not by chance! We did not come into this world unnoticed! The Universe accepted us precisely at the right time and the right place. You did not enter the world of flesh by accident! One of my favorite passages in the Old Testament is found in the Book of Ecclesiastes 3:1-8:

There is an appointed time for everything,
    and a time for every affair under the heavens.
A time to be born, and a time to die;

a time to plant, and a time to uproot the plant.

A time to kill, and a time to heal;

a time to tear down, and a time to build.

A time to weep, and a time to laugh;

a time to mourn, and a time to dance.

A time to scatter stones, and a time to gather them;

a time to embrace, and a time to be far from embraces.

A time to seek, and a time to lose;

a time to keep, and a time to cast away.

A time to rend, and a time to sew;

a time to be silent, and a time to speak.

A time to love, and a time to hate;

a time of war, and a time of peace.

What advantage has the worker from his toil? I have considered the task which God has appointed for us to be busied about. *He has made everything appropriate to its time*, and has put the timeless into our hearts, without us ever discovering, from beginning to end, the work which God has done.

You are not an accident! He has made everything appropriate to its time, even your birth and all the main events in your life. What is not determined is your response to life! Your free will, plus God's Grace, decides your destiny.

13. BELIEF IN THE PARANORMAL

I have never seen the slightest scientific proof
of the religious theories of heaven and hell,
of future life for individuals
or of a personal God.

—Thomas Edison

I realize that this book may raise a few eyebrows. Whoever heard of a priest talking about paranormal activity? Anytime I used to mention the topic to some of my friends, they would just stare at me *as if I didn't have a second floor!* It is not easy to discuss a subject, such as the *paranormal.* For some reason, it is usually prejudged negatively by those who do not understand its true meaning.

Webster's New Collegiate Dictionary defines the word *paranormal* as "something not explainable by science." Random House Webster's College Dictionary gives this definition for the word paranormal: "Of, or pertaining to, events or perceptions occurring without scientific explanation, as clairvoyance or extrasensory perception." Given that understanding, practically everything a person *believes on faith* would be considered paranormal. It would include anything that takes place in church, from reading the Bible to singing hymns that touch on the spiritual life. It would include prayers, novenas, devotions and miracles, since what happens on these occasions cannot be explained by science. A person, in prayer, is talking or praying to someone who is not physically present and communicating with a person who is without a material body. That is *not* a normal conversation between two persons. It is beyond scientific proof.

Also, expecting to go to heaven is a paranormal desire, since there is no proof that heaven does exist. That is correct! Who could prove that heaven is real...scientifically? Yet, most of the persons I have met during my lifetime believe in the afterlife. The belief is consistent: heaven is living a life that is far superior and far more beautiful than this one. Heaven is the Kingdom of God, which is more real than this world; it is the goal that fulfills our life in a way that is beyond anything we can imagine.

St. Augustine says of our destiny: "Our hearts were made for Thee, O Lord, and they cannot rest until they rest in Thee." The average Christian—or a member of any religion, for that matter—learns, as a child, to accept the concept of being rewarded or punished for our actions in this life.

The Detroit Free Press stated that the average American is a believer in God and God's Kingdom of Peace and Happiness that will last forever. In fact, about eighty percent of Americans believe in God, and about fifty percent have had some kind of mystical experience, or communication of some sort, with a loved one who died.

I was always interested in science and religion. In the late seventies, I became interested in, and pursued my certification as a Lecturer in the Silva Method of Mind Development and Stress Control. I was especially attracted to it because it *combined both science and religion.* I came to realize that if a person believed only in science, it could easily lead to atheism. On the other hand, if one were overly pious or religious, such a person may very well become a religious fanatic. The extremes are always dangerous. Balance between the two extremes is where reality is found. This was the key to the success of the Silva Method. After achieving a great deal of success as a Certified Lecturer, I decided to offer the Course to my fellow priests in the Archdiocese of Detroit. My first action was to place a notice in the Archdiocesan Newsletter—sent to all the priests.

Seventeen priests responded. I had no idea whether or not the Course would be acceptable to a group of Roman Catholic priests. There was only one way to find out. I had hopes that the support of fellow priests in teaching a Course that touched on Metaphysics would encourage other clergy and religious to pursue such studies.

The priests were very attentive and cooperative with every part of the program. They had no difficulty with the conditioning cycles (meditations), or with any of the basic scientific, subjective or spiritual principles upon which the whole Course is presented. Dr. Jose Silva, a devout Catholic himself, and founder of the Silva Method, had done extensive research on every aspect of the copyrighted material, verifying his premises with scientific data. (This great human being, Jose Silva, moved on to the spirit world early in the year of 1998.)

The religious input depended on each Lecturer. I combined both science and religion in my lectures. Regardless of the religious background of my audience, there was never any particular religion that was viewed with disfavor or criticized. On the contrary, one's beliefs were reinforced through the phenomenal experiences of those taking the Course. Well over eight million people have taken the Silva Method, and all of them either had an incredible psychic experience or witnessed one first hand.

At the end of the Course taught to the priests—and one bishop, I might add—I passed out an evaluation sheet to each graduate present. There was an overwhelming approval to every question. There were six questions on the evaluation:

1. *Did you enjoy the Course?* I was surprised and delighted by the positive responses I received. Every one gave a strong affirmation. They seemed to be genuinely excited about the God-given *abilities* and *gifts* given to every human being.

2. *Do you think it would be helpful in Pastoral Ministry? If so, how?* Almost everyone replied that the techniques learned in the Course would help them in their prayer life, and in serving others more effectively. Some added that it helped them to understand Sacred Scripture more deeply, especially in the area of healing. Also, that the Course gave them the tools to be more compassionate.

3. *What part of the Course did you find most helpful?* The answers varied, but the most popular responses were: learning the techniques for Relaxation, Problem solving, and a more Focused Concentration in meditation and prayer. Understanding Mind Expansion and Mental Projection were also well received.

4. *Would you recommend another priest to take the Course?* Everyone put down a "yes." In fact, they were hoping that the Silva Method would be taught very soon again. Some had already convinced other priests to take it whenever it would be offered.

5. *How best can the Course be presented to priests in order to encourage more of them to take it?* The most common recommendation was to include a monthly statement in the

Archdiocesan Newsletter—also, by word and example and by encouragement. They preferred taking the Course in three or four consecutive days in an intensive setting, rather than three or four hours a week for ten weeks (That was all the time I could spare having been assigned, at the time, to Holy Trinity, an inner city Parish, where we spent almost the entire day—every day—in continual service to the poor and needy.)

6. *Is there any part of the Course, when given to priests, that should be omitted?* All said "No", except two of the participants who said the talk about the *theory of reincarnation* could have been better used on the *prayer life* of priests or *meditation.* (I gave a presentation on the possibility of reincarnation and how perfect justice could be served. For example, if someone were deeply prejudiced against the people of another race or culture, perfect justice would be to come back as a person born into that race or culture. That would certainly solve the problem! And with no fire, damnation or force!) But I thought that only two objections on a single point was an excellent percentage, considering the participants were all Roman Catholic priests.

The failure on my part was to continue teaching the Silva Method to priests separately. I did continue to teach the Silva Method for fifteen years, whenever I was able. In fact, I taught the Course over sixty times to the general public. Priests and nuns were always welcomed to take the Course. And some did!

But, as always, women are more apt to take such a Course. Many nuns took the Course and loved it. At almost every session, there were always some Religious Sisters present. And they always spoke favorably of the Course.

Priests and nuns are very open to *understanding* God's Word, as given in Sacred Scripture, but also how the Word of God can be *applied* to daily life. Persons who have dedicated their lives to God are aware, more than most people, of God's abiding Presence. They know it, they teach it and live it to the best of their ability. It was, therefore, quite easy for them to accept the basic principles of the Silva Method, such as having a healthy self-image (remembering in Whose image we were created), psychic diagnosis or ESP in which we can communicate mentally with each other. That should be an easy concept to accept, since clergy and religious believe in the Spiritual or Mystical Body of Christ in which we are all joined together in spirit.

The *paranormal*, in the final analysis, seems to be *normal*!

14. ON BEING RELIGIOUS, SPIRITUAL OR BOTH

In the middle is found
balance and power.
—St. Thomas Aquinas

Being a priest for more than forty-three years has taught me a lot about human nature. I have often reflected on how I have changed through the years—especially in my attitude. What am I learning about myself, as I live to the best of my ability, according to the laws of the Church? Do I live a life in perfect obedience to the laws established by the religion I embrace? Even more penetrating, how do I respond to the Laws of God as I understand them?

These are questions I hope all of us can address, regardless of which religion we are talking about. The following statement is not an opinion, but rather a fact: Many people have changed their loyalties from one religion to another. They are raised in the religion of their parents, but they decide, at some point, that another religion would be closer to their personal beliefs. In the last forty-three years, I have prepared hundreds of persons, of various ages, to accept the Catholic Faith in place of their previous beliefs and upbringing. Whenever this happened, I always admonished them to first learn about the religion in which they were raised before giving it up for another. That particular belief system, in which they were born, was given to them for a reason. As I continue to affirm, I don't believe in accidents—not with an Omniscient (All-knowing), Infinite God of Love who has created all there is. On the other hand, living in linear time, we feel surrounded by accidental happenings.

I did not say that a person, taking classes to become Catholic, should not change religions. I simply said they should know enough about their prior religious beliefs before they accept another set of beliefs. I joyfully welcome them into the Catholic Church! If the change from one religion to another is a step forward, deepening one's relationship with God, then it is to be highly recommended. It is a wonderful transition from a static relationship with God to a dynamic one, one that radically transforms a person into a religious and spiritual being on a path that bonds deeply with the Creator.

There are, of course, a surprising number of people I have encountered in my priesthood who have left the Catholic Church and joined another religion. Again, I would ask the same question: did they actually study the Catholic Church well, before leaving it? Was it only a child's view of the church they were leaving? I find it interesting to speak with someone who left the Catholic Church and joined a more modern church—without naming any of them—in order to build their relationship with God. I have to chuckle sometimes when I hear of some people leaving the Catholic Church because they are upset with some of the beliefs or practices...which no longer exist! Even more amazing are the ones who leave and are totally unaware of the impact of the Second Vatican Council, which, in the sixties, updated the church and placed it in the modern world. The Council rewrote many church policies, laws and disciplines, and especially helped to redefine Christian attitudes, by promoting fresh interpretations of Scripture and removing ancient or obsolete practices and traditions.

Pope John XXIII, who called the Vatican Council, affirmed that it was time to *open the window and let some fresh air in.* He was referring, of course, to a two-thousand-year-old church which had grown heavy with policies and practices that were no longer functional in the modern world. I, for one, was delighted to see such an important updating of a worldwide religion. The Vatican council, with the Bishops of the world present, went through a complete self-examination in front of religious leaders of other denominations. It was a bold move! I don't know of any other religion which has done this, or even contemplated performing a complete spiritual *overhaul* in the presence of other religious leaders.

Yet, any religion, updated or obsolete, of itself is not enough to bring a person to spiritual peace and happiness. A person who is only *religious* is not necessarily spiritual. This is the dictionary's definition of a religious person: "one who adheres strictly to an institutional body of laws, observances and beliefs." This being so, that is why there are hundreds of different religions in the world, each claiming to be the right one. Just adhering to any particular religion is not enough! A person also has to be *spiritual*. By that, I mean one who follows the *spirit* of the law rather than the *letter* of the law. An overly religious person takes things literally without thinking, without questioning, without understanding, without application. We would call it *blind faith!* On the other hand, a spiritual person respects human conscience, spiritual values and lives a life of doing good and avoiding evil.

Here are some examples of what I mean. While I was assigned as Pastor of Most Holy Trinity Parish in downtown Detroit, the following took place right after Mass. I was taking some things off the altar when I noticed that there was only one person in church—a very devout lady in the front pew. She was reciting her rosary after Mass as she did every day. Just then, one of the *Knights of the Road*, (a street person) came in and sat down quietly in the last pew. The lady saying the rosary got very upset and moved quickly down the aisle, still saying the rosary. When she reached the man sitting in the back, without warning, she immediately began to beat him over the head with her purse—and a good sized purse! She kept hitting him over and over, yelling: "Get out of my church. You don't belong here. Get out!"

I ran down the aisle as fast as I could. I had to drag her away from him. I called her by name, saying, "What are you doing to this poor man?" Before she could answer, I said, "This is not your church. It belongs to the people, not you! Now go back and finish whatever you were doing!" This is the picture of what I saw: she had a rosary in one hand and the purse—used as a weapon—in the other. I was alarmed and horrified. I apologized to the poor fellow who was obviously frightened and told him to continue praying or resting...if he wished. This elderly lady went to Mass every day, said her rosary at least once a day, usually before, during and after Mass. She had just received Communion, and she was in the House of God. I know this is not a typical example! It is, in fact, quite extreme, but it does demonstrate the obvious difference between being religious and being spiritual. She was obviously religious—overly religious—but lacking terribly in spirituality.

Perhaps another example will throw more light on what I am saying. I had a friend who left the Catholic Faith and joined a very fundamental religion which took the Bible very literally. He maintained that, if it's in the Bible, it is absolutely the Word of God—every word, as it is written. (He was referring to his English Version of the Bible, even though the Bible was originally written in Hebrew and in Greek.) He never questioned anything. It was blind obedience to the letter of the law rather than the spirit of the law. One day while we were discussing his favorite subject, the Bible, he quoted Mark 16:15-16, in which Jesus says:

> Go into the whole world and proclaim the Good News to all creation. The man who believes in it, and accepts Baptism will be saved; the man who refuses to believe in it, will be condemned.

My friend, taking everything literally, maintained that all those who are not baptized will go to hell forever. I replied that, according to the Almanac, there were over four billion people who were not baptized. "Would you put them all in hell?"

"Yes!" He affirmed, and without any remorse! I asked him if his own mother were not baptized, "Would she also end up in hell?"

"Of course!" he came back quickly, without blinking an eyelash. I said to myself: *Either this guy is the cruelest person in the world, or he is the most ignorant!* I decided that he was the most ignorant and most misguided person I had ever met. He is no longer with us. I hope he finds some spirituality (enlightenment) on his journey in the next life! I am sure he will be surprised at the kind of people he sees inhabiting the Heavens. The Catholic Church wisely understands the necessity for Baptism, but explains that there are three ways to be baptized: by water, by blood or by desire. The use of *water*, by pouring, sprinkling or immersing, plus the words of the Baptismal form, performed in the name of the Father, and of the Son and of the Holy Spirit, is the most common way. A *desire* to live a life that is moral and honest, and following one's conscience in the performance of good works, also merits salvation, regardless of what persuasion he or she embraced. The third way is by *sacrificing one's life* because of one's Faith or sincere convictions, such as a martyr's death.

Although most of the members of any religion do not hold such rigid and fanatical views of the Holy Scriptures as my friend above, there are many who do arbitrarily interpret certain passages literally and use them as a weapon to condemn. I personally know—and I am sure you do, too—dedicated members of a religion who choose to quote sacred texts to their own advantage. They will condemn others of another faith, quoting freely from the Bible and making wild judgements about other people's belief system or their styles of living, and condemning them outright, ignoring another Bible quote that says: "Do not judge, lest you be judged." Contradictions in belief are not obvious to everyone.

Again, some Christians are in favor of war and capital punishment but are strongly against abortion. Does this make any sense: "You can kill adults, but not infants?" Or they may be violently against suicide or assisted-suicide but continue to be a chain-smoker, drink heavily or eat fatty foods that can clog the vascular system and cause heart attacks—all of which are a slower form of suicide. Not that all deaths are attributed to these causes, but they often play a role in one's early demise.

The ideal human being, in my estimation, is one who has achieved a balance between the religious and the spiritual. The number of authentic believers in today's world are on the increase. They may or may not belong to a mainline religion, but they are aware of basic Divine Laws and live an active life in the service of others.

Mother Teresa is a good example of a person who was very religious and very spiritual. She continued to remain a nun all her life, joyfully attending Mass and Communion every day, saying her rosary with her Religious Community and fulfilling any other devotions expected of her. She became famous because her life work was caring for the homeless, the sick, the dying and countless others in hopeless situations. The world had already canonized her a Saint before she was called to Heaven. *Balance* was her strength. She respected God's Law diligently and devoted herself to the spirit of the Divine Law: *To Love God and love your neighbor as yourself.*

Martin Luther King, Jr. was a minister of his own church and a spiritual leader of the African-American Community. He was able to keep a balance between the set of religious beliefs and observances of his denomination and, at the same time, champion the cause of millions. The spirit of the law was to reach out and enter the struggle for equality and freedom. He had gone to the mountain top, he was free at last...and paid the price that is demanded of most prophets. In the centuries before Christ, most prophets all met the same end: an early death, because there was always opposition to change—even if it were for the better!

Princess Diana, in my estimation, was another spiritual giant who kept a good balance between the letter and the spirit of the law. She was a member of the Royal Family by marriage. There was a traditional and fixed pattern of behavior expected of the Royal Family. This she respected, but she was also open, as well, to the spirit of English Law and tradition. She was able, in her capacity, to reach out beyond London and touch the lives of many thousands wherever she went. This was possible because she broke through obsolete traditions and identified with the common people and their human rights, supporting their causes. She even gained worldwide attention because of her ability to belong to *Royalty* and to *the people* at the same time.

Jesus, of course, is a primary example. He represents to Christians, the highest spiritual life possible in this world. At the same time, He continually aimed at purifying religious observance.

He paid the temple tax and was often found in the Temple

teaching. He also knew the Law of God more perfectly than anyone else in human history. Yet, it was the spirit of the Law that He proclaimed in his brief, but very effective Ministry. He kept Laws and observances that promoted holiness and rejected the obsolete ones. He was opposed because He did not encourage His followers to perform the ritual washes before eating. This does not sound important today, but at the time Jesus lived on earth, it was enough to bar Him from the Temple. It was the letter of the law that He objected to, as if the washings cleansed the soul. Actually, He rejected laws that emphasized an *outward cleansing only.* Jesus said it was much more important to *cleanse the inside of a person* from which comes evil. The outside is only the result.

He also infuriated His opponents when He broke obsolete laws: He spoke to a Samaritan woman in public, and He drank a cup of water from her hands, both of which were forbidden for a devout Jew in those days.

What really irked His opponents even more was healing on the Sabbath. It's hard to imagine, but *healing* was considered *work*—as if they all could do it!—and they were furious with Him for healing.

Here is the incident in which Jesus healed on the Sabbath, breaking another obsolete tradition. (Matthew 12:9-15)

He left that place and went into their synagogue.

A man with a shriveled hand happened to be there, and they put this question to Jesus, hoping to bring an accusation against him: "Is it lawful to work a cure on the Sabbath?" He said in response: "Suppose one of you has a sheep and it falls into a pit on the Sabbath. Will he not take hold of it and pull it out? Well, think how much more precious a human being is than a sheep. Clearly, good deeds may be performed on the Sabbath."

To the man he said, "Stretch out your hand!" He did so, and it was perfectly restored; it became as sound as the other. When the Pharisees were outside, they began to plot against him to find a way to destroy him. Jesus was aware of this, and so he withdrew from that place.

Today, it would seem totally insane to refuse to heal someone, just because it was a particular day of the week. Unfortunately, this was one more obstacle placed in the Master's path.

The relationship with God is maintained...and that is the purpose of all Divine Law. Today, people in all walks of life are making their own moral decisions, especially when it is a personal matter. They used to run to the *Answer Man*—their Pastor—and seek counsel to assist them in making the best moral choice in a given situation. Of course, some still do, but the numbers of parishioners, who follow their own path, are growing rapidly. This is obvious to any priest! Very few confessions are heard today compared to the past. At the same time, there are more Communions today, percentage-wise, than before the Vatican Council. The movement seems to indicate, rather clearly, that faithful Christians are becoming less inclined to traditional obligations and more open to life as it unfolds...that is to say, less sin-conscious and more spirit-conscious.

15. TRUTH IS A PATHLESS LAND

If a man does not keep pace
with his companions,
perhaps it is because
he hears a different drummer.
Let him keep step to the music he hears,
however measured or far away.

—Henry David Thoreau

How we approach God through our way of life is unique to each one of us. There are no two people in the whole world who see life identically. There are no two fingerprints that are perfectly identical, nor do you find the iris of the eye or the thought-patterns of any two people exactly the same.

People of every religion have a different set of truths or doctrines. That is what sets them apart. At the same time, members of the same religion have their own private and personal beliefs about what is truth. One person's truth is another person's superstition. Truth is quite elusive: If one can imagine a spectrum with millions of degrees between *Absolute Truth* and *absolute falsehood*, there would be no two people sharing any single degree on the entire spectrum of truth. We were created *equal,* but not *identical* in the eyes of God! We all have a name, distinctive characteristics and unique qualities. In a sense, we are like snowflakes, quite similar, but not exactly alike.

As we discussed in the chapter on prayer, each of us maintains a unique relationship with God. That remains true for the rest of our lives here, and the Divine bond will continue into the Realms of Eternity. Unfortunately, we identify with our upbringing and culture in this world, in preference to our cosmic and timeless origin in the Mind of God. We are usually blinded by our mortality and physical limitations, putting aside—often, for many years— the truth of who we are. This is entirely normal for a human being living in two worlds: one that can be seen, felt, touched, and the other which is invisible to the physical senses.

Naturally, with the above being so, we are quite vulnerable to the influences around us from our earliest childhood. In fact, it is impossible to grow up in a vacuum, that is, without any outside influence altogether. We learn the language of our parents before we can read or write. Without realizing it, we adopt the culture, religion, customs and values of our parents and the environmental surroundings in which we live. We live and talk like people around us, and, in a sense, share similar views about the world, the weather, politics—and usually root for the same home team in sports. None of the above is new.

What may be new is the invasion of *fresh ideas, which flow from our own experiences* or the experiences of others. Children born in modern times, are subject to, and strongly influenced by new ideas seen on television—both good and bad! The cultural influence begins to weaken.

Then comes the introduction to books that offer many new concepts foreign to the cultural surroundings of our early life. If our thirst for knowledge continues, we find ourselves in a typical bookstore, flooded with new books every day...books that are as varied as life itself, covering every topic imaginable: namely, books that are spiritual and inspirational or, to the contrary, books that are shocking and revolutionary; then, there are some that offer self-help or self-improvement methods. There is no limit to new ideas! Improving our lives and the horizon of our interests is symbolic of the modern times in which we live. It does not take long to realize that we are different from any other person in the whole world, although our goals and our problems may be similar. In a word, we all share the same desire, which is to be better than we are. Goals, however, are not easily achieved, because the effort must be personal and the path is unique.

Self-questioning is universal. Questions are always flashing through our minds: "How can I feel good about myself?"

"Why am I so unhappy?" I have been trying for years and

nothing happens. And if I do lose a few pounds, why do I put them right back on?"

"How can I get out of this financial mess I'm in?"

"I am starting to get angry more and more easily, and more often; what's the matter with me?"

"*I go to church* every week...it doesn't seem to help. I am still unhappy."

"Maybe, because *I don't go to church* I am so unhappy."

"Why does God allow the world to be in such a mess?"

People who are religious and people who are not religious, have the same questions they have been asking themselves for centuries. It comes down to: *"What's wrong with me?"* And it does not matter one iota, whether a person is wealthy or poor, professional or amateur, young or old, educated or illiterate, and regardless of the color of their skin, they ask themselves the same questions. Wealth does not automatically bring happiness; poverty does not either. In fact, nothing outside ourselves is the actual cause of our joy or our sorrow. However, the *interpretation* of what happens outside ourselves does make a big difference. In fact, it makes all the difference in the world!

Years ago I heard a short poem that summed it up quite well:

Two men looked out from prison bars;
one saw mud, the other saw stars.

Each of us sees a different world out there. To some, it is a very hostile world; to others, an enchanting planet, teeming with life and natural phenomena. Happiness is a point of view, a choice. We all respond or react differently to situations, even to the same situation. If ten persons went to the same baseball game, they could easily give ten different opinions of the game, such as:

"It was the best game I ever went to."
"The worst game I ever saw."
"About average," and so on.

We also find, in our differences, that some of us are weak and some strong. A point in fact: some people would be destroyed by an accident that left them in a paralyzed condition. Just having one hand or one arm paralyzed is enough to leave a person in a state of despair, with no space for happiness in their lives. Yet, that is not always the case, because each of us is different!

Take, for example, Darryl Stingley who had been a wide receiver for the New England Patriots in the seventies. He was severely injured in a game against the Oakland Raiders and was paralyzed from his chest down...with no hope of recovery. He could only move one hand. With that one hand, he is able to move around in an electric chair...to this very day! Has he despaired? Cursed the Lord that gave him life? Not at all. In fact, Darryl insists that, in some ways, his life today is better now than in his former days. He made an unusual statement about his football days that makes us pause in wonder at the greatness of this man. Here are his own words: "I had tunnel vision. All I wanted, was to be the best athlete I could and a lot of other things were overlooked. Now I've come back to them. This is a rebirth for me."

This is a positive testimony of what could have been interpreted as an unbearable tragedy. I am sure that another person with the same physical injuries may give an entirely different viewpoint. We are all faced, at one time or another, with a choice of how to interpret certain "troublesome" situations and problems.

There is an old saying: "We do not see the world *as it is*; we see the world *as we are*." As a matter of fact, everything we see out there is interpreted by us. We can see a beautiful world, a paradise, a Kingdom of God or we can see a *hell-on-earth*, an ugly place, a God-forsaken planet. It's all in the eyes of the beholder. We see what we *want* to see...what we *expect* to see.

Being a clergyman gave me a lot of experience. I helped many people, but also, during that time, I learned a great deal from *them*. People who are experiencing pain or terrible discomfort are great teachers!

The books I read and my position as Pastor offered me

excellent opportunities to assist a parishioner, a relative or a friend in overcoming a difficult situation. I was *helper* and *listener* at the same time. I did not want to give the impression that I was preaching to those who were hurting by bringing up one Bible quote after another. The Bible has its place, but no one wants to be *preached at!* Rather, while counseling, I combined counseling techniques with other sciences I had learned from workshops and seminars throughout the years. It was my opinion, and still is, that to make a change, we have to deal with the *whole person*, not just the external problem at hand. If the change is not holistic, it is short-lived!

Modern psychology and parapsychology have thrown much light on the subject, through a deeper understanding of the mind and its different levels. There is also an increasing awareness of the wide complexity of the total person. In modern times, a human being may be seen through many perspectives: the social, physical, spiritual, psychological, intellectual, emotional, intuitive and religious, to name a few. Somewhere in these dimensions, there is present the source or cause of happiness or unhappiness in every man or woman.

There are psychologists, therapists, psychiatrists and counselors who have been advising and assisting people for many years. And they do a fine job of helping their clients achieve peace of mind. To follow their line of assistance is always open to everyone and is well recommended.

As a clergy person, I have always continued to explore the many aspects of life that cause pain and suffering, joy and peace. Along with the use of Sacred Scripture, I have been interested all my life in the various Sciences. It is a wonderful gift to have faith in the Scriptures! Nevertheless, in today's world, there is a place for what we called, in a previous chapter, the *paranormal,* along with some measurable proof. We may also benefit from the evidence called *The Wisdom Of The Ages,* passed down to us by our predecessors, who have paved the way for advancement in every field of learning—through an actual experience and the accumulation of knowledge. Their discoveries have stood the test of time and are also a great help in understanding the totality of a human being.

Since we are all different in so many ways, we all view our Divine Parent in as many different ways. Not all religions agree to the understanding of Absolute Truth.

Two thousand years ago, (John 18:36,37) Jesus affirmed that His Kingdom did not belong to this world, Pilate responded:

"So, then, you are a King?" Pilate replied.

"It is you who say I am a King.

The reason I was born,

the reason why I came into this world,

is to testify to the Truth.

Anyone committed to the truth hears my voice."

"Truth!" said Pilate. "What does that mean?"

This ended their conversation.

The quest goes on. *What is truth?* There is personal truth and there is Absolute Truth. God *is* Truth! My belief is that Jesus taught Truth in the highest sense of the word. Those who do not profess the Christian Faith may not agree with me, and that is okay! I am not the last word on God's Truth. Others may believe there is no Truth that is Divine and all-encompassing. We all have a free will to choose the truths we wish to live by. The dictionary defines truth as *conformity to fact or reality.* If my truth conforms to my sense of reality, I will establish that truth as a conviction, doctrine or law by which I guide my way of life.

For some, the Bible is the last word on Truth; others will say the Koran or the Hindu Vedas are God's Truth. Truth is a pathless land. When we consider the population of the earth at approximately six billion and rising, it would be cruel and unrealistic to think that God has only called a small percentage of the human race to Himself. Rather, it would seem much more reasonable that God has called His children from every religion and every walk of life to follow a path to their Divine Source. We were created as individuals, each reflecting some attribute of God—and not production-line, machine-made robots. God apparently loves variety. The billions of forms of life on this one planet testify to that! The flowers, the trees, the animals, the insects—including people of different races and colors—are clear evidences of a highly imaginative and Creative Power. Besides what is observable, we have no idea what is going on throughout the rest of the Universe.

Does not each person have a right to seek his or her own Source, Origin and Giver of life? We can't even get to step one in conveying our truth to another if there is a language barrier—with no one to translate. Why should a person of a different culture, language and history accept our truth as better than theirs? Again, I say, truth follows many paths to the Creator. There is no clear map that transcends the serious differences between races. Missionaries have done a great work in converting native inhabitants to Christianity. But what about the other four billion who are not baptized? Are we going to put them in hell, as my friend who translates the Bible literally, would suggest?

I like what Isaac Bashevis Singer once wrote:

> Life is God's novel.
> Let God write it.

Shirley Beaupre of Most Holy Trinity used to say something very similar, "Why can't we let God *be* God?" We try so hard to reduce God to a prejudiced, narrow-minded, bigoted creature like ourselves. We have things reversed. God created us; we did not create God! The path the *so-called pagans* choose is perfectly known by God, and, in some mysterious way, must be inspired by the same Spirit of Life—leading them through other channels to Almighty God. The truth of it is that God is the Creator of our worst enemies, the biggest trouble-makers and the most dangerous arch-criminals in the world. I am not trying to justify them...not by any means! If they have a conscience that knows right from wrong and still follow their evil ways, they condemn themselves. When I say that God's Truth is a pathless land, I am not saying that *wrongdoing* is the same as *rightful action*! Free will is given as a perfect gift to choose right knowledge, right speech, right behavior, right effort and right mindfulness to name some of Buddha's Eightfold Path of enlightenment—which can be summed up as truth in action or truth applied. And we are all given such opportunities to achieve salvation.

Beneath the concept of truth is a love that also comes from God and is one of God's attributes. God is One, Love, Joy Truth, Goodness and Peace. There are many more attributes which can be applied to an Infinite Being—and they are all interchangeable because God is *One* and *Everything* at the same time! Love and service are the keys to spiritual growth. Those sincerely seeking truth include love and an appreciation of goodness as the motive and basis for their actions.

The Dalai Lama also sees the connection between God-like behavior, love and enlightenment:

> The reason why love and compassion
> bring the greatest happiness
> is simply that our nature
> cherishes them above all else.
> The need for love lies at the very foundation
> of human existence.
> It results from the profound interdependence
> we all share with one another.

16. WHAT IS *REAL* IN THE WORLD?

Science without religion is lame.
Religion without science is blind.
—Albert Einstein

We are being *bombarded* today, from every direction on the *Information Highway,* with knowledge in every field imaginable. So what does a person do in the face of continual exposure to information both good and bad and with lot of grey in between? I can only answer: with *discernment and discretion!* A suggested line of action would be to begin with one's *ideals.* One's *value system.* One's *beliefs.* If not, then one's direction in life gets shaped by what is *out there,* rather than by the *spirit within.*

I have chosen to put into print my thoughts and reflections on the experiences I have had and the impact they have made on my life. I have tried to keep in mind what little I know of Universal Law and the Principles of Truth as found in the Sacred Scriptures. The more I seek, the more I am affirmed by the knowledge of others' experiences very similar to mine.

Reflections on my personal history means an encounter with mystical experience and paranormal activity. Through no deliberate effort of my own, I have walked a path that was filled with surprises, far beyond my expectations, accompanied by altered states of consciousness. Along with these experiences, came some incredible, measurable results and I was given, more than once, a glimpse of the realities beyond the limits of physical sight. Yet, it is not easy writing about *invisible realities.* I know my statements will be met with some skepticism by a certain percentage of my readers. I can't blame them! If I did not experience them, I, too, might wonder about their authenticity.

However, I do have one advantage. Since I was a child I have not only had the *faith of believing in the unseen,* as St. Paul would put it, but of having verification displayed before my very eyes. I am referring to the vision I had with three of my siblings. Later in life, I was happy that my siblings witnessed what I did, reassuring me that *something real* was happening before us. Besides, I grew up in an environment with parents and a family of deep faith, who nurtured a profound and unwavering belief in the Divine Presence of a Living God—a God Who is continuously active in all that is created. In addition, as a clergy person, I have had the fortunate experience of expressing my faith and personal reflections every weekend throughout my priesthood in various pulpits of the Detroit Archdiocese.

Each expression of faith reinforces it. What we believe

becomes a way of life, not just a package of laws, statements or religious opinions. I have read in a book, published by *The Foundation for Inner Peace,* that: "We *teach* what we want to *learn.*" I am in full agreement with that statement! I have done that all my life. Whenever I wanted to learn a new system of thought or a new technique, I would start a group in which we would study and discuss what we all wanted to learn. That is precisely what we did when we studied a book called: "A Search for God," published by the *Cayce Foundation.* The same thing occurred when I taught Mind Development Courses and Stress Control. There is a strong need to internalize, through study and discovery, the techniques or knowledge we wish to share with others. The pattern remains the same: always teaching what we desire to learn.

I wish to learn as much as possible about God and God's involvement in our life. I often read what I can about theology, which is the study of divine things and religious truth. God's Truth is Eternal, and from the viewpoint of Eternity, anything temporary is illusion. What is accepted and believed today is gone tomorrow. We are accustomed to making idols out of anything man-made. We make great efforts to find stability and permanence in something that cannot last. Nothing is as it appears to be. That is why each religion has its own personal theology, which is the foundation of its belief system.

The concept of reality is always changing when based on

the physical senses, which are fragile and different in degree for each of us. Some people see better than others, taste more sensitively than others, smell more acutely than others, etc. Sometimes, our reality is based on nothing more than hearsay or faulty tradition. At times, it is our firm belief in science that forms the basis of our reality. However, science changes also.

Let me explain. At one time, the "true reality" was a volcano which was treated like a god, who got angry once in a while and destroyed villages...later the sun was worshiped. Still later, as in Egypt, there was a family of gods and godlings. At one point in the history of Ancient Egypt, an unusual Pharaoh by the name of Akhenaton, tried to establish only *one God* as the Creator of all things. He was met with great opposition. He was, by many centuries, ahead of his time. He was not only rejected, but his enemies—those committed to the old ways—tried to erase from history, whatever he taught about one God and whatever good he accomplished in his lifetime.

To the Hebrews, there was the God of Moses Who delivered them from slavery, but for forty years, there was continual complaining and longing for the good old days. The reality of a new belief in God and achieving freedom was not easily accepted. Even though they experienced the famous exodus from Egypt, they were still unsure of their new reality.

The pursuit of reality goes on. Those of you who were alive as long or longer than I, can recall that building a nuclear bomb with its massive destruction was unheard of and not even mentioned in our science books at any level of education—that is, not until Hiroshima and Nagasaki were destroyed. Not until the sixties, did we come to believe in space travel. Flash Gordon was a fantasy and nothing more! Then it happened! The Russian Sputnik orbited the earth, awakening the entire world from pure imagination to stark reality. Added to our exciting revelation, in June of 1969, we sent a man to the moon. I am sure you remember the first words spoken from the moon: "One small step for man, one giant step for mankind."

Our reality changed overnight! All over the world! Science became a god! Later, the Computer Age opened up another world, right here on planet Earth. We never heard of nor dreamed, that a new kind of machine would make the typewriter obsolete. Science was now on a roll! Soon the Internet was put in operation, making the Information Highway accessible to the young and the old, opening up a whole, new world in which ideas could be learned on every topic imaginable or messages exchanged immediately through an incredibly fast electronic mail service. Enormous hard drives and sophisticated software accompanied the computer year after year. New computers became obsolete quickly as chips turned from kilobytes to megabytes to gigabytes...and now, terabytes.

My point should be clear. Science changes with every new earth-shaking discovery...and so does our reality. We often hear today the same expressions that refer to one's truth: "That's *your* reality, not mine!" or "This is *my* reality!" The reality we are talking about is not Absolute Reality. Only what is *Real* in the sight of God is Absolutely Real, just as personal truth is not necessarily God's Truth!

We had no idea how many moons orbited Jupiter until recent probes were sent there. Galileo only saw three or four of them. It was enough to convince him that the earth was not the center of the whole Universe. Today, we know of about a dozen more moons orbiting Jupiter.

We used to think that the only way to cook was on a gas or electric stove, besides a grill or hibachi. Now, a microwave oven is found in almost every kitchen. Bachelors like myself are delighted with it. We can heat up yesterday's food in a few moments. People working hard all day can heat up a meal for the family in seconds, while doing something else. The microwave oven has revolutionized the American way of cooking.

Children today are born into a different reality than the one we older folks remember. Times are changing! Reality is changing! The realities we often hold on to, no longer exist. This is true, not only in science or politics, but also in the medical field, in which the most sophisticated, high-tech equipment has radically altered the whole process of medical diagnosis and surgery.

As far as education is concerned, people in some cities are getting fed up with old methods of teaching, using books that are outdated or out of touch with today's latest discoveries. You would not expect to see changes in one's religious beliefs or dogma, but the discoveries of certain ancient cities, manuscripts and artifacts throw new light on our understanding of religious beliefs in the first millennium. Vatican II demonstrated clearly how necessary it was to update a two-thousand year old church.

Another new item: Many States have now become lawsuit-conscious. Lawsuits were almost unheard of in my early years. Today, a good Samaritan type of individual is afraid to assist someone injured in an accident, for fear of being sued by the very victim he or she is trying to help. Discipline in some schools is almost non-existent. I had my hands whacked with a stick in my primary grades. Some teachers even tried very hard to make me write with my right hand; I was one of the few who continued using my left hand. Today, teachers would be sued in a moment, if they disciplined with physical contact or tried to force a child to switch hands. Reality moves on...and so does the perception of truth.

The strict sense of past morality is now causing older folks to experience some distressing eye-openers at the behavior of the younger generation. Among other things, the younger folks often use *words* or live a *lifestyle*—You don't need an example!—that shock older people. New math scares older people. And we did our homework without a calculator!

So, if reality keeps changing, what, then, is *True* and what is *Real* in the sight of God? We have remarkably accurate sources to draw from: Sacred Scripture and Tradition! (The Word of God *written* and the Word of God passed on by *word of mouth*.) We need Eternal Truths to understand Eternal Reality. Jesus speaks of Eternal Truth: "Heaven and earth will pass away, but my Words will never pass away." The teachings of Jesus about God and the way to happiness are still true! Two thousand years have not changed what is Eternal.

Jesus is the Way, the Truth, and the Life. We can become aware of Absolute Reality through Him. Also, Moses and the prophets spoke of God to the people of their time. They often delivered messages of warnings and reprimands, concerning the behavior of the people at that particular time, but when the prophets were truly prophetic, speaking on behalf of Yahweh, their teachings also remain true through the corridors of time. They also gave a very clear and complete description of the Messiah, who was to come into the world. Christians believe that Christ fulfilled every detail of the Messiah's life as predicted by the prophecies of the Old Testament. In Him is found Truth and through Him is Salvation achieved, although there are many Christian religions which differ greatly in the interpretation of these truths. There may be *one* Christianity, but there are about sixty different Christian religions in the United States. They are further divided into one hundred and forty-five denominations. Why is this so? Because they all share the same posture: each religion has its own package of beliefs which they sincerely believe is their path to salvation.

Our Jewish brothers and sisters have a different reality. They are still looking and waiting for the Messiah to make His appearance. We should not be alarmed since their Tradition precedes Christianity by nearly two thousand years and therefore, quite expectedly, differs greatly from the Christian perspective. In the world of Islam, Jesus is highly respected as a prophet, but not Divine. Many oriental religions, on the other hand, focus on the teachings of Buddha, who lived about six hundred years before Christ.

We are still choosing our personal reality today. Each of us has a distinct approach to God and a separate slate of rules, regulations and beliefs. People claim to have the Truth, with absolute fundamentalism on one end, and absolute freedom on the other—with countless viewpoints in between. Truth, beauty or reality are still *in the eye of the beholder.*

In the 1998 Almanac, we find that, in today's world, grouping all Christian religions together, there are about two billion believers or one third of the human race. That's impressive! But I was surprised to note that there are between two and three billion people on this earth today who do not profess *any* religion. Millions, according to the Almanac, are downright anti-religious and oppose religion in any form.

How do we find our way in such a mess of religious confusion? Again, where is Reality? What is Real and what is temporary or imagined? The answer to these questions, I don't know. I adhere to the Roman Catholic religion, because I personally believe it to be the closest to Reality among all the religions of the world. And there are many to choose from. I do not wish to offend my reader in any way, but that is my choice, my reality, if you will! Your choice is your reality. And I respect your choice! We all have the same ultimate goals in mind and just belonging to a particular religion does not assure us of being on the right path.

I am sure that everyone reading these words have acquaintances that are faithful church-goers and other acquaintances that are not. The difference is not always obvious. And sometimes, the unchurched are more God-like than the ones attending weekly religious services. My point is that God touches the life of all His children without exception. We are equal before God, but we all respond differently and in very unique ways. Reality has many faces! When we get to the place where we think we have the whole Truth, and nothing but the Truth and all others adhere to false beliefs, there is a very important factor to consider: we judge by what we see and by what little we know, whereas God judges the heart, the seat of genuine, God-like activity. Our view of another's reality needs a lot of adjustment.

I attended a funeral this morning for Bettie Dawood. She was a good friend and benefactor of Most Holy Trinity church while I was Pastor. I knew some things about her, but I had no idea how many activities she was actually involved in—I mean activities on many levels: parish life, city projects, state issues and an active participation in some national projects. Besides the public life of this extraordinary person, she was very generous to causes for the poor and the homeless, through some charities unknown even to her own family. These were brought out by one of the six priests who concelebrated at her well-attended funeral service. I learned a lot about her, and I am sure there is much more.

Edmund Ahee is another friend who died recently. His truth and his reality were simple and clear: he spent his time, his personal involvement and a generous portion of his income serving the poor and the homeless. He was well-known in the Detroit area for his generosity. Yet, there were many other gifts he demonstrated that were shared at his funeral. Only God knows the whole story of each person's life.

We know so little about each other!

I have conducted hundreds of funerals. It is amazing the information that comes out when a person is called to heaven. No one's whole life is an open book. We only know bits and pieces about one another, if that much! Funerals often bring out surprising details of another's life, which may or may not be complimentary. Shakespeare reminds us that

> The evil that men do lives after them;
> the good is oft interred with their bones.

That also happens in our day. Some presidents, who died recently, have had their reputations tarnished by writers who wish to offer *the rest of the story*. Those negative details make us wonder what is real and what is not...what is the truth, since it is forever changing.

Making comments about another person's life often includes many *statements* and many *judgments* used freely as if they were interchangeable. Although we are told not to judge, we are not discouraged from making statements. The difference between the two is important, since one is a real picture and the other is, at most, a guess—the latter usually distorting or condemning the image of another human being. An example of making a statement would be the following: There are two brothers. Bill is sixteen and stands five feet ten; his brother Jim is only ten years old and several inches shorter. To say that Bill is taller than Jim is a perfectly good *statement—very* true and very real. However, to say that Bill is a better person than his brother is a *judgment*. In God's eyes, we do not know that!

Another example: to say that, in general, an African-American person is darker than your typical Caucasian is a statement of reality. To say that one is better than the other is a judgement and *unreal*. Only God is able to judge accurately, because God has access to all of the facts about every single person in the world—something we can never achieve in this life. And thank God, that God is much more loving and forgiving than we are! *After all, God loves His six billion children unconditionally...that's the real picture.*

I am not referring to our Court System in which, according to law, a judgment or sentence is given, after all the "facts" are presented to the opinion of a jury, which is considered a decision. These are strictly legal matters and justice is executed according to Civil Law not Divine Law. Mistakes are possible because of human limitations.

On Judgment Day, I suspect the first question asked will be: "How much did you love and serve without looking for anything in return?" In other words, "Did you love unconditionally?" I like the way St. John of the Cross put it:

In the twilight of life,
God will not judge us on our earthly
possessions and human successes,
but on how well we have loved.

PART FOUR

Many of my concerns and reflections have to do with what I know about the mind, its importance, its responsibility and its function in this mysterious creature called a human being.

I believe that is what attracted me so much to the Silva Method of Mind Development. It seemed to encompass what I was seeking at the time. I had no idea that programming the mind and putting the mind to work through programs and conditioning cycles empowered the mind to become more effective and to achieve its goals and purposes. Even a person well versed in human anatomy may be lacking greatly in the operation of the mind. I really get excited when I address the whole question of meditation, mystical experience and awakening the power of the Spiritual Centers.

The remaining chapters will all cover some aspect of meditation. The topic is much too big for one chapter. As a matter of fact, a whole book would be more adequate. I pray that these few ideas will at least be helpful in your meditative pursuits.

17. MEDITATION

> Meditation...to go from our conscious
> through the unconscious
> to the experience of
> Pure Truth or God.
> —Diarmuid O'Murchu

When we speak of meditation, we are talking about *guidelines* more than *experiences*. Experiences are too personal and unpredictable. I can only speak of the many ways people reach God. They are all legitimate and real. Sometimes, there are similarities, sometimes, not! Since there are no two people exactly alike spiritually and mentally, we can only receive accordingly, as an individual. I will emphasize that meditation (as well as prayer) deserve the full length of a book (or books), but since I am simply writing my *reflections*, I pray that my experiences will be helpful not only to the experienced meditator, but also to those taking their first steps on the meditative path. Please do not expect to receive what I have received. Nor can I expect to live your experience. Uniqueness is one of the qualities the Creator gave each of us when He brought us into being.

At times, it is difficult in this world to remember that "All is one" in God and that we are never separate from God. Meditation helps an *individual* to move closer and closer to the reality of this oneness, wholeness...holiness.

Meditation is even a little more difficult to define. Among the various definitions, we may say that meditation is the "kenosis" or "emptying" oneself of anything that prevents the Creative Forces of God from elevating our awareness to the highest consciousness within us. I have more to say about this in the chapter, *The Power Within.*

Meditation is not reverie or daydreaming, but rather attuning the dynamic energies within us to their Spiritual Source. It is, therefore, the awakening of our mental and spiritual forces to a point of expressing and experiencing our relationship to God...*this is true meditation*—it is not just *believing* in God, but *knowing* God...the latter being far superior. In prayer we speak to God, in meditation God speaks to us. The results are tremendous. The silence of all outward and earthly distraction and of all distracting thoughts are essential if we are to hear God's Voice. It may not be an audible voice, but you will get the message pertaining to your quest and your purpose, including the circumstances and concerns of your life. Your path becomes more defined and more certain after communicating with God in this manner.

Prayer and meditation are companions to one another, like two sides of the same coin. Prayer expresses a desire for a deeper relationship with God and a greater knowledge of God! When we show our Divine Parent that we strongly seek guidance and help, what follows is an attitude of waiting, of expectation, of silence and of listening to be able to hear the soft and nearly inaudible whisper within, and to know that all is well.

The old translation of Psalm 46:10, "Be still and know that I am God," is a good start on the narrow path that moves forward and upward toward the heavens. Only when we are *still* may we know God, and in that unutterable silence is our soul prepared to say and mean with the Master, "Not my will, but Thine be done!" It is then that we also share St. Paul's affirmation: "I live now, not I, but Christ lives in me."

I read a lot in the Seminary and continue to do so. I devoured many books on prayer, continually discovering new ways of communicating with God. Meditation is one way, with its many methods and techniques, of how to *listen* to the Voice of God. They are simply an idea about God, until one actually experiences the truth of it. *Knowing* and *being there* are the ultimate experience of creature to Creator. In fact, *knowing* and *being there* is everything! There are many definitions of meditation, the most popular one being the one mentioned above: *listening to God*. That is clear and simple, but there is so much more! Another definition may be that *meditation is a process, in which we become aware and experience the highest thought imaginable, of who we are and who God is.*

Obviously, meditation is experienced in many forms. What I now see is a broad spectrum with the *very simplest* method of meditation all the way to the *most profound*. They all had results, producing some spiritual benefit. Goals and intention are the *heart* of meditation!

Meditation is the key to bringing heaven and earth together as one, with no separation. There is no "God out there!" and "We here!" It takes a lifetime to realize and to own the truth that we are God's Family. When we meditate, we remember that very important, overlooked fact that we share in God's Nature, since we were created as one of God's children.

I do not intend to give all the basics of meditation, such as you would find in a text book. I can only relate my story and my experience. The process has to begin somewhere. The year I began to board at the Seminary, I started to meditate. I was 15 years old. Just a young teenager! Regardless of my age, I found much consolation, spiritual growth and, to a degree, enlightenment according to my needs and values at that time. Later, I began making changes in the system and technique used in meditation, and also in my purpose and direction.

While I was still in my teens, I meditated faithfully, but I did not realize at the time what kind of meditation I was experiencing. I simply thought that my simple meditations were the real and complete thing! I had heard of Saints having incredible mystical experiences, but I thought, at the time, that God only granted the Holy Ones that privilege. It would be arrogant to think that Almighty God would intensify my meditations with such incredible experiences.

I would call the type of meditation I pursued in the Seminary, a meditation of the *intellect*. That kind of meditation analyzed a problem and offered the means necessary to resolve it. Being problem-oriented, it was marked by analytical reasoning, or in simpler terms, a consideration of the problem, or topic from every angle. In this manner, I would have a clearer grasp of something I did not like in my behavior and how I could change it. For example, since I was a student living in the Seminary, a meditation on *obedience* would bring to my awareness a review of obedience according to Seminary policy and rules of behavior. If I wanted to practice perfect obedience, I would focus on my shortcomings in regard to keeping the rules, let's say, regarding silence after evening prayers in which there was silence until the next day. I examined my conscience. Did I speak at night to one of my buddies in the hall or in the common, large lavatory where we would brush our teeth at the sinks, side by side? Did I break the grand silence on my way to morning prayers? Continually monitoring oneself is a powerful way to improve one's life.

This type of meditation for an average adult can also be very productive. It is a way of monitoring one's behavior. Heart monitors serve the same purpose in the area of health. In the meditative state, you can ask yourself: "Why am I gaining weight?" You begin to analyze: "Do I go for snacks every time the commercials come on television, especially when it advertises some delicious cake, candy, sandwiches, pop tarts or countless other tempting delicacies?"

Actually, the average person does not need a commercial to move into the kitchen for a snack. Just watching TV encourages it. Usually, it gets boring just sitting there! And there is so much repetition.

Then, there are the other areas of life. Are your foods high in fat grams, calories, sodium or carbohydrates? Do you look at the "read-outs" on the outside of the product, indicating the composition of the food you intend to put into your stomach and which will affect the total body system? You can see that improvements can come quickly, if one is serious about self-improvement.

Of course, you can spiritualize this form of meditation by examining just how often, or how rarely, you talk to God. Going through an entire day, a typical day, just how often do you take the time to address your Divine Parent, Who loves you more than you love your children? You may even question,

"What is most often on my mind?" "What do I spend most of my time thinking about, being concerned about—actually, what is my number one priority?" "Is it time to prioritize...to reconsider...to make changes...to re-visit my values...to analyze why I am so unhappy or bored or depressed?" Any one of the above is worthy of a meditation!

Let me move ahead. There is a form of meditation in which you can use *guided imagery* to hold your attention and make a change in your direction. For many years in the Seminary, my meditations sometimes focused on the imagery of Christ's experiences. For example, during Holy Week, the last week of Jesus' life on earth, I would visualize, as clearly as I could, the whole Paschal Mystery...that is, the suffering, death and resurrection of Jesus.

I would recall in meditation how He was badly treated by the soldiers, who whipped Him, spit on Him and made fun of Him: "*You're* a prophet! Tell us , who struck thee?" I would also meditate on the *whole* experience of Jesus, bringing home to me how I contributed to His need to die, out of love, on a cross. But the Easter meditations were glorious, beautiful and exciting. I enjoyed imagining the Risen Christ in all His Glory. Naturally, one can make a good meditation about any Biblical character, such as Moses, Abraham, the Mother of Jesus, Peter, Paul or King David.

There is another kind of meditation that can be helpful to a person who desires changes of any kind: at work, at home or simply a change in attitude. To borrow from the Silva Mind Development Course, it is called the Mirror of the Mind. This is how it works: with your eyes closed and looking—not straight ahead—but a little above the plain of sight, visualize first, what you do *not* like about your situation: the fear, the anxiety, the hurt, the stress, the discomfort, the anger, and so forth. You picture—with color, location and specific details—all the things you do not like about your particular conditions at home or outside the home. Then you mentally burn that picture, destroy it somehow and never go back to it. Then, to the left of where that image was located, now imagine what you *would* like: possibly a raise, working in a different part of the building, having a different boss, returning to a peaceful home after work, having the best day of your life or getting along joyfully and peacefully with your spouse, the kids and the neighbors.

This is a powerful method of meditating to change the circumstances in which we live. Don't underestimate the power of visualization and its impact on life. You are putting your subconscious to work! More on that later. Such imagery brings clarity to our deepest desires and motives. It can bring peace in your home. You can achieve a much higher and more desirable level of awareness, in which you find yourself. It is your option to choose what is important to you.

There are other forms of meditation which are directed to problem-solving. They are all helpful, but they do not necessarily lead to spiritual growth, nor do they have to. Nonetheless, they *do* work and can enhance one's living conditions. However, the most important quality a human being can experience is being fully alive and spiritually awake! Any form of meditation that leads to spiritual growth and a greater perception of reality is worth pursuing. Pick a method of meditation that suits you best.

From the time I was ordained a priest in 1956, I continued to meditate but felt as if it were not enough for me. I wanted more! I desired to seek out some methods, that have been tried and tested, from the greatest meditators in the world. At that time, I still put the Saints in another category. They died, I thought, and took their *spiritual recipes* for meditation with them. What were people still alive saying? I recall so vividly, walking at night in Holy Cross Church, asking for help in this manner. At first, I was only *asking*! Then, after a period of time, my words became stronger...I *pleaded* for help. Months later, there I was walking around the church at night, in the dim light of votive candles and now, *demanding* some action. "You are *God*! You're supposed to be *helping* me! *Where* are You? *What* are You? Are You listening? I need something more! My ideals are slipping past me. Please don't let that happen! Guide me! Show me a path that will work. Something real! I want to know You more intimately. I desire more than anything else in the world to *experience the nearness of You*. Please, Lord, hear me and show me the way!"

The above was not a one-time prayer; I would go through prayers like that night after night, walking around and around the darkened church, in and out of one aisle after another. At times—I have to admit—there was almost anger in my voice...as if I were being *cheated* out of something I should have. And my voice was by no means silent. I was even yelling, at times, amid tears and sweat! Much of what happened is covered in my first book: *On My Way Home*. I do not wish to become repetitive, so I will simply say here that I continued to condition my body and mind with basic Hatha Yoga breathings and postures before I began to meditate.

My first meditations were affirmations, such as:

"I love you, my Lord!"

"My Jesus, mercy!"

"Fill me with your Divine Light!"

"The Lord is my Shepherd; I shall not want!"

There were many affirmations. I tried to keep it simple. This went on for years!

At times, I would just sit in meditation. I wish to state this clearly: in my opinion, it was not the Hatha Yoga (posture and breathings) that was important; otherwise, everyone who wants to meditate deeply would have to practice Yoga. That is not so! It was the *intention*, the *determination*, the *persistence*, the *passion*, and the *conviction* motivating me that gave power and meaning to my actions.

In 1968, I added some new techniques to my preparation for meditation. While at St. Bernadette Church, I meditated several times with one of my co-workers: Sr. Kathy Peatee. We had gone to a workshop on meditation. It stressed the discipline of focusing the mind and removing all distraction. It was recommended at the workshop to light a candle, stare at the flame, try not to blink, then close your eyes. (This was only a suggestion. We took it seriously.) The first thing we both noticed was that, as soon as we would close our eyes, the image of the flame from the candle dominated the darkness. The image was beautiful to look at, but it was in an opposite color than the actual flame and started to move off center and drift away. The power to focus then was exerted. Mentally, we had to move the light back to the center and keep it there. This took will power and determination. Try it! After a while, I had no difficulty keeping the image of the candlelight in the center. I would even move it around to wherever I wanted it to go. This may be a good *step number one* in training the mind to focus on one thing and one thing only!

I continued to study about the importance of the deep breathings as an integral part of the preparation for meditation. I learned that the air we breathe is not just plain old air, but *chi*, which is the breath of life, in the same sense that we call God the Holy Breath. That is what the words *Holy Spirit* means: *Holy Breath*!

Another method of relaxation for the serious meditator, is to tighten, then relax the major parts of our anatomy. For example, tighten the foot and ankle area, then relax them; then the thighs, then the torso, the arms, the neck, the eyes...each time, holding the tension for a few moments, then releasing totally all tightness or stress from that part of the body. It's surprising how totally relaxed one can become. This is not the meditation; rather, it is only a preparation to condition the body so that its energies will work *with* you, not *against* you. If you feel very exhausted, stressed out and tense, you are not in the right frame of mind for meditation. That is why the body needs conditioning first.

Of course, all of the above is secondary to the conditioning of the *mind*. Mental distractions are far more disturbing to the effort of focusing on one thought or of clearing the mind of all thought. The latter is the most difficult, but the most beneficial;

the result is the silent mind, the most powerful mind in the Universe. But that comes later!

It is commonly believed that we are composed of body, mind and spirit. Borrowing from Edgar Cayce, the mind is the mediator between the spirit and the body. In fact, his point of view is that *the spirit is life, the mind is the builder and the body is the result* or manifestation in this world. I quite agree with that. Our spirit cannot function in this world without a mind. As unfortunate as it is, Alzheimer's disease occurs when the mind is no longer functioning properly. And when someone acts totally out of order, a friend may say: "Have you lost your mind?" The mind could be our greatest friend or worst enemy. If one's mind is terribly troubled, it will be difficult to calm down, to relax and to think clearly. Even the most extraordinary person has to work at focusing the mind.

I recall, at times, I felt ready for the meditation, when suddenly, my mind was filled with questions, "Did I lock the front the door...or the door of the car...or leave the lights on in the house, etc.." Some people have mentioned that they wondered if they left the stove on, some other electrical appliance or maybe left some meat on the table. Many thoughts *cross* the mind when you *least* want them: "Was I rude to that person at work?" "Did I say *thank you* to the person who gave me a surprise gift today?" "Was it starting to rain/snow when I came in?" "Did I get things ready for my guests tomorrow?" "Did they remember?" "Should I call first?"

The list of questions, good thoughts, disturbing thoughts, distractions of every kind seem to pop up, when you are training yourself to quiet the mind. It is not a bad thing. It merely demonstrates how the ordinary mind is quite busy...and undisciplined! After a period of time, the serious meditator is able to relax both body and mind and is open to the higher mind or to the spirit created in the Divine image. When you get to that point, you have come a long way. And when you are *there* you will know it; there will not be the slightest bit of doubt.

The benefits of daily meditation are many. Better health, improved self-image, greater self-confidence, reducing hypertension, achieving goals, pursuing one's highest ideals, setting up the possibility of having mystical and spiritual experiences and actual healing are all within the grasp of every human being through meditative efforts. The *ultimate goal* of meditation, however, is similar to the goal of prayer. *Prayer is a relationship with God; meditation deepens that relationship.* The results are truly unlimited and the positive effects are staggering; yet, it does not cost anything, but a little effort and time.

18. KNOW THYSELF

How many more idols must you find

before you realize

that you are the one

you have been searching for?

—Dan Fogelberg

"Know thyself" is the beginning of wisdom. This has been stated by Plato and all great philosophers for centuries. This is not a *suggestion*, but rather a *necessity*!

To begin the pursuit of self-knowledge there only are two requirements demanded: *A sincere desire to seek the Truth and a consistent willingness to move forward.*

Meditation does not have to be long, but rather be consistent! "Seek *first* the *Kingdom of God*, and all these things will be given you besides," said the greatest Master of meditation. And where did the Master Jesus say the Kingdom of God is? As I am willing to repeat often, "The *Kingdom of God is within you!*" Is it not logical to begin the quest for truth by turning *within*? Many people have been looking for answers to their basic questions about God, life, purpose, and so forth, from others, from books, cassettes, videos, from lectures...*from anywhere outside themselves* and come away still asking the same questions. The answers are God-given; they came with the package, so to speak: being created in God's image. The *knowledge* of who we are and the *purpose for our existence,* were included in the *gift of life. Discovery* of the truth is simply *remembering* the truth within.

The ultimate goal of every human being seeking truth is a greater awareness of God and who we truly are in our relationship to God. Anything less than that strays from our ultimate purpose in being created by our Divine Parent. Proper preparation of body and mind, and consecrating ourselves in prayer, humility and a contrite spirit is the path of enlightenment. Then, when we call out in meditation, the answer will be given. Attunement to the Divine or Christ-consciousness is very possible, once the right decision is made. Recall what was said in the Old Testament in the Book of Joshua: 24:15, "Decide today whom you will serve...as for me and my household, we will serve the Lord." That statement was serious and was meant as a life-long decision.

There is much said these days about *the road less traveled* or the narrow path. That path is very rewarding even in this life, but it does demand some discipline and a higher level of awareness. It is easy to find oneself moving off course, knowingly or unknowingly.

We live in a world of *instant gratification.* There are many electronic appliances that make it possible. Remote control of the television set, the remote garage opener, microwave ovens, electric can openers and many more items are within reach of the typical American family. We also have quick ways of getting where we want by car or by plane. We can also connect faster by telephone or through the Internet, with its countless forms of on-the-spot communication, including e-mail services. Life can be filled with information, knowledge and electronic correspondence without ever leaving home.

To ask someone to practice some form of discipline that would interfere with any of the many forms of communication that gratify us does not go well usually. To advise someone to go within, to find the answers they seek, does not usually impress the listener. And so, to request a continued, daily, ongoing, consistent effort to know one's self, one's purpose and one's place in the universe through meditation, loses its appeal for a good percentage of people in America. The goal is *very attractive*, but *time* and *patience* are usually lacking! It is quite the opposite of *instant enlightenment* or *immediate results* through electronic equipment or some other outside mechanism. It would be so much easier just to read about meditation, watch a program about it on television or surf through the Internet for answers. On the contrary, meditation is definitely a hands-on, do-it-yourself experience!

Only in recent years has rapid progress been made in the understanding of how the mind works...and we have only started! As I understand it, there is only One Mind—the Universal Mind of God. All minds simply share in the great Mind of God. We are told that we are created in the image and likeness of God. Strangely enough, I still meet people who believe that their physical body is included as God's image and likeness. This cannot be so! The physical body can never be modeled after Pure Spirit! It would be a contradiction. As Jesus said to Nicodemus in John 3:6, "Flesh begets flesh, Spirit begets spirit!" Only our *spirit* and *the higher mind*, through which the spirit functions, are created in the image and likeness of God. God's Infinite Energy (Spirit) functions through His Infinite or Universal Mind and His Divine Will. We are only a *tiny spark* of God's Infinity. Nevertheless, we are highly complimented when both the Old and the New Testament say *we are as gods*. Jesus, Himself, testifies to this.

The word mind can be confusing, since we speak of the conscious mind, the subconscious mind and the superconscious mind. Are there three minds? No! There is only *one mind* seen from three different aspects.

Let's begin with the conscious mind, which is the most familiar. It is the conscious mind that we use from morning till night each day, in our awakened state, because this aspect of mind is needed to function properly in this three-dimensional world. The conscious mind is a powerful commander of the forces within us. However, on the negative side, the conscious mind is quite limited in its views. It came into existence when we were born, and it grew up with our body, learning from the five senses and other outside input—what life is all about. It is also associated with the ego, because of its focus on the lower self and the personal belief that its total self, including body, mind and spirit, is separate from all others. The ego, or conscious mind, tends to be quite narrow, fundamental and distorted, because of its limitations of thought and rejection of unseen realities. Notice on page 235, the diagram demonstrates how little the conscious mind knows—it is compared to the tip of an iceberg (upside down), in which the bulk of the iceberg is hidden. In the same way, most of our knowledge is hidden in the subconscious and superconscious mind.

Egos clash all the time. Family feuds, violence, war and every sort of conflict stem from two or more limited-thinking egos engaging in a confrontation over values or a point of view. The conscious mind insists on winning all the time. *I win, you lose!* The conscious mind tends to be selfish, rude, intolerant and demanding. The list is much longer. I am sure we all have met people that, unfortunately, fall into the above categories.

One of our greatest blessings is having the subconscious mind as part of human life. The subconscious mind, another aspect of mind, is truly a god-send. Our personal subconscious mind has thousands of jobs to take care of, including all of the involuntary activity of a human being to stay alive, such as maintaining and regulating: the heartbeat, the blood pressure and circulation, the lungs and breathing patterns, the digestive system and much more that we are not aware of, as we live and breathe each day. At the same time, our personal subconscious mind is also our servant, our biocomputer, that is capable of fulfilling almost all our wishes...within reason.

The amazing computer is modeled after the subconscious mind. Just as you put software into a computer to operate a particular program, we do the same with our subconscious mind or biocomputer. If negative thoughts are believed and repeated frequently, such as "I will never amount to anything in life!", a command has been programmed. It will be fulfilled as the *master* insists! You may not realize it, but your conscious mind is the *operator*, the *boss*, the *big chief* giving orders to your incredible biocomputer—for good or for bad! Be careful what you say and mean, especially when said with emphasis. The biocomputer like an electronic computer only does what it is commanded *literally*! So if you say with emotion,

"You make me *sick*!"

"That really *kills* me!"

"He is a *pain in the neck!*"

"He is a pain in the behind!" (You may have other words...)

"I am *sick* and *tired* of your excuses!"

"That kid (or my mother-in-law, my job, my neighbor) will

be the *death* of me yet!"

I think the point is made.

If repeated, serious illness or consequences may follow! (And we can't blame God for this one!) An interesting example that is true, but quite sad, is what happened to one of my students, when I was teaching Mind Development. A young lady got up and shared her story. She said her favorite expression was "I can't stand it!" A few years later she developed the most unusual condition: a bone started growing on the bottom of her feet. It became so painful to walk on either foot that she required surgery to remove the bones that appeared—in a sense, out of nowhere. She said the doctors were totally amazed. They performed the surgery, but Medical Science could not explain the cause. At least, not by the book! The real villain was the conscious mind repeating a negative statement to the subconscious mind, the faithful servant which fulfills the master's every command.

Another true story: a business man (I will withhold his name) was told by his boss that he had to move to Chicago, because of some downsizing that was required by the company. He had nothing against the city of Chicago, but all his family, relatives and friends—his whole life—was situated in the suburbs of Detroit. Mainly, his heart was there. He was soon on his way to Chicago by train. He hated the thought! It became so heart-rending to leave home and unbearably painful to take up another life that there was only one way out. He died of a heart attack on the train, midway between the two cities. He had been in excellent health up to that point.

There are many examples of tragic consequences that follow strong negative programming. On the other hand, we are also able to have positive thoughts with positive results:

"I will wake up tomorrow morning feeling better than I have felt in a long time!"

"I will awaken at 5:20 a.m. tomorrow!"

"I will be calm when I see the doctor tomorrow!"

"I no longer need to smoke!"

"I no longer need to nibble on food between meals (or eat candy, red meat, or drink too much!")

Please understand this process correctly. Just because you say these things, does not mean they are going to happen. You must first ask yourself if you are serious about making changes in your living habits and are you accustomed to making suggestions to your subconscious mind and *expecting results*? If not, your incredible servant, the subconscious mind will probably respond: "Are you talking to me?" or "Look who's talking?" Confidence and trust must be developed first!

Try something simple first, such as, "I will awaken at exactly 6:30 a.m. tomorrow morning!" When you are able to awaken at any hour you choose, then move on to something else. *There is no limit to what you can accomplish if you are making firm suggestions without any doubt, whatsoever, and conforming to God's Law and the Universal Laws* set in motion by God.

If someone questions this process saying, "Are we not supposed to have faith only in God?" I would answer, "Yes!" However, God is all. God is everywhere. There is nothing *outside* of God. All power in heaven and on earth, and throughout the Universe, is God's Power. There are many ways to put God's Power into operation. We put faith and trust in our parents, in the Constitution of our country, in our teachers, in our churches, in our conscience and in our religious leaders. Can we not put faith in ourselves? Why would we lack confidence and faith in the *subconscious mind* that formed our body, according to the blueprint of genes and DNA. It is the same mind that is *still in charge* of maintaining life and giving us the help of God when called upon. St. Paul reminds us, "We know that in all things, God works for good with those who love Him..." Our life evolves and unfolds according to our desires and goals and to the more spiritual person...our ideals.

Faith, without any doubt whatsoever—the size of a mustard seed—is enough to bring about healing, even when it seems impossible.

You have the ability to remove fear, worry or anxiety; you can overcome a bad temper and improve your health condition. You can be peaceful and happy, regardless of what is happening around you.

When parents have children, the children, being of the same nature as the parents, are able to function in the same manner as the parents. Being God's children, we, too, are creative to the extent that we are able to function as co-creators with our Divine Parent. Faith in God and faith in oneself go hand in hand.

Jesus said to the blind man asking for help, "Receive your sight. *Your faith has healed you.*" Seven different times in the Gospels, the Lord clarifies that it was their faith that healed them. The Master even affirms in Mark 11:22-24:

Put your trust in God. I solemnly assure you, whoever says to this mountain, "Be lifted up and thrown into the sea," and *has no inner doubts, but believes* that what he says will happen, shall have it done for him. *I give you my word,* if you are ready to *believe that you will receive* whatever you ask for in prayer, it shall be done for you.

He adds, in St. Matthew's Gospel, "Nothing would be impossible for you." Actually, it would take a whole book to understand this tremendous power that is available to us. Read Dr. Joseph Murphy's book "The Power Of Your Subconscious Mind." It is really a classic on this subject. There are also many other books that deal with the miraculous servant (subconscious mind) available to us.

Allow me to share with you a miraculous event that took place in Dearborn Heights, MI. On November 21, 1998, I was invited to the home of one of the parishioners of St. Mel's Parish. She had also invited Barbara, a guest I did not know personally, but may have seen in church. Barbara asked me if I would bless her...which I did, of course. She was filled with confidence of success and her faith and trust in the Lord were strong! She felt comforted by the healing/blessing I gave her, but she knew it was God's Power we draw on to work the miraculous. Unknown to me, Barbara was about to have surgery for a very large ulcer that was threatening not only her stomach, but her life as well—if it became cancerous. Four times she had undergone an EGE. If you are as curious as I was, it stands for esophogastroduodenoscopy. The results were clear! The ulcer was unchanged and was still a threat. Surgery was arranged for December 7, 1998 at Garden City Hospital. Dr. Spinale performed the surgery.

During the operation, there was some confusion. Dr. Spinale could not find the ulcer. While in the Operating Room, the surgeon called the other doctor who had taken the x-rays. Once again, he was informed exactly where the ulcer was, and so he returned to the operating room and looked again for the ulcer. He still could not find it. He then requested the doctor, who had performed the tests on her, to come to the Operating

Room...which he did. Together, they still could not find it. Both doctors are ready to testify that it was impossible that the ulcer of this size and nature could have healed in such a short period of time. The operation was successful, except that nothing took place, but the revelation that God is still active in the world. Doctors are normally not accustomed to call something miraculous. This case was an exception!

They sewed her up and sent her to her room; the doctor expressed total amazement. She told the doctor she was not surprised at all. A priest had blessed her and she believed she was healed...and she was. Was it my blessing that brought about the healing? I do not think so. It was her faith in God that would make her well, even if it took a miracle to do it. Her faith set up the conditions for the impossible to happen. It did!

The subsconscious mind received the message of complete trust. God blessed that prayer, as requested. There is another aspect to the subconscious mind. It is not limited to our bodies only. All minds are connected through the subconscious and it is possible to access this network of minds. ESP is based on this premise. Psychics are able to pick up information about a person they have never met before by attunement to that person's subconscious. In the Silva Method of Mind Development, millions of students who have taken the Course, were able to tap into the subconscious mind of a particular person simply by being given the name and city of that person in mind. This is called psychic diagnosis because the diagnosis of a sickness or an unhealthy condition is detected from a distance. It does not matter where that person is on the planet. They zero in on the right person out of billions of possibilities. The success rate is phenomenal! This has all been researched and documented!

Again, my discovery of how the subconscious mind works occurred to me one day, as I was driving to the northeastern part of the city of Detroit. It was in the morning and I started to daydream, watching the sun and the morning clouds. Without realizing it, I had gotten off the freeway at the wrong exit. Trying to get back on, I made a couple more wrong turns. Now, I wasn't sure where I was going. I found myself retracing my tracks. I stopped for a moment and thought about it. Then I realized I was not far from the home of a couple that I knew for many years, but had not seen in a long time.

I decided to surprise them with a visit. When the wife came to the door, she was not surprised at all! She said, "Thank God, you got my message!"

"What message?" I fell back in complete surprise!

"I called you on the phone this morning," she replied.

"You must have phoned after I left the Rectory." Then it dawned on both of us, that somehow I got her message without the phone call. Our minds were connected on a subconscious level, as are all minds. What a great gift and power resides in each of us. It is difficult to imagine any mind greater than the one just described.

Yet, the superconscious mind/higher mind is far greater in scope and ability. It is normally not in contact with the material world. The spirit energy functions through the Higher Mind in a dimension beyond this three dimensional world. *The Higher Mind is always in Communion with God.* If we could see our spirit and the higher mind, we would probably mistake it for God and fall on our knees in worship. We really have no idea of our greatness. A Divine Parent produces offspring with divine qualities. Although we are merely a point of consciousness or awareness in the Universal Mind of God, there is no question that we come from Divine Stock.

To communicate, know or experience the higher mind or our inner spirit, we have to rise above ourselves and ascend to its spiritual level. This I will take up in the last chapter. The diagram of the six pointed star on page 236, represents the approximately six billion people living in the world today. Each of us has a conscious mind like the tip of the iceberg. Hidden within is the subconscious mind, which include imagination, creativity and memory. Beyond that is the higher mind and the spirit, created in God' image. We are joined with one another and with our Divine Source. This is heaven on earth. This is oneness. This is Home. Here is the place where we belong. Unfortunately, there is little or no direct communication between our conscious and our superconscious mind. Some people, unfortunately, never become aware of this godly force within us in their whole lifetime.

My Prayer List
(print names only)

_____

_____

_____

_____

_____

_____

_____

_____

_____

_____

_____

_____

Thank You, God.

Yes, I will join you in heart and mind during World Day of Prayer on Thursday, September 13, 2007.

United in prayer, I will affirm with you:

We are peacemakers, one in the love of God. With hearts united, we establish harmony and peace in our lives and in the world.

Name _____

Address _____ Apt. _____

City _____ State _____

ZIP _____ Phone _____

E-mail _____

☐ Send me the World Day of Prayer information packet.

☐ Please remember these people in prayer on September 13, 2007 (Please print):

_____

Use reverse side for additional names.   DWD-8-07

Tear off and send to: **F7839702**

unity® 1901 NW Blue Parkway
Unity Village, MO 64065-0001

To submit your prayer lists and prayer requests online, visit *www.worlddayofprayer.org*.

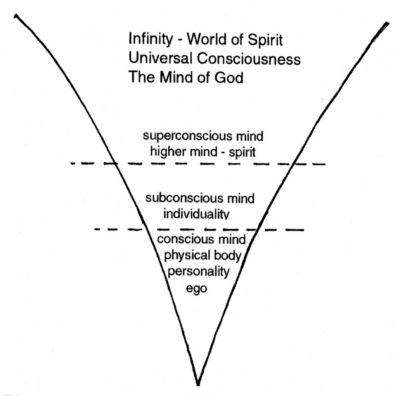

Infinity - World of Spirit
Universal Consciousness
The Mind of God

superconscious mind
higher mind - spirit

subconscious mind
individuality

conscious mind
physical body
personality
ego

Diagram 1: The Mind of God compared to our limited minds.

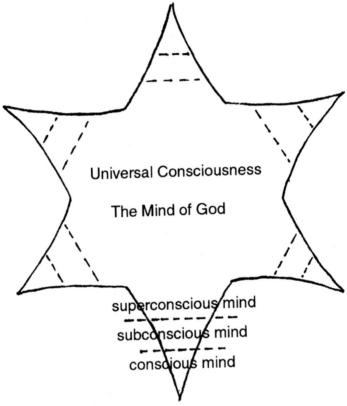

Diagram 2: Six-pointed star signifies 6 individual persons. Multiplied, it actually represents the 6 billion persons on the planet.

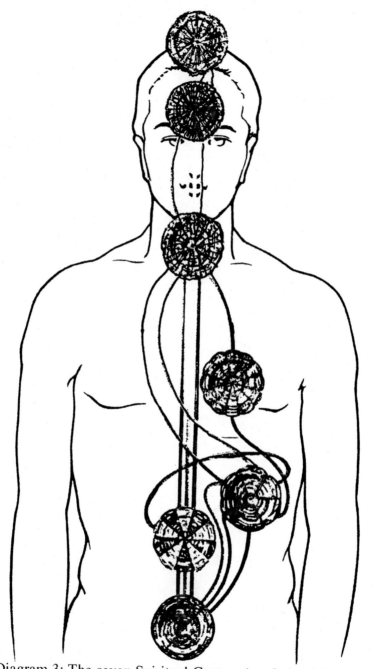

Diagram 3: The seven Spiritual Centers (or chakras) in every human being.

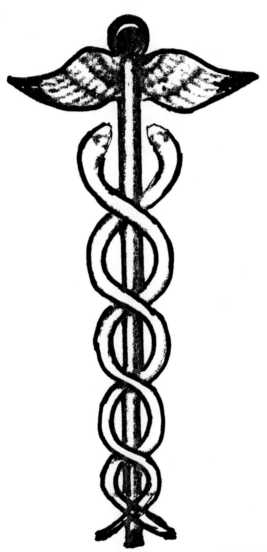

Diagram 4: The Caduceus, or Medical Symbol. Originally, this was a symbol of healing through meditation.

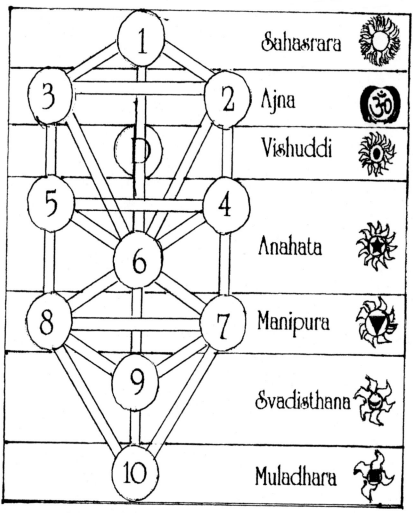

Diagram 5: The Sephiroth: the Tree of Life.

239

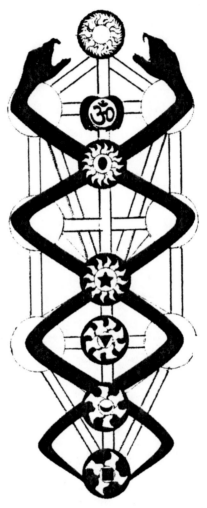

Diagram 6: The Spiritual Centers imposed on the Tree of Life, according to the Cabala.

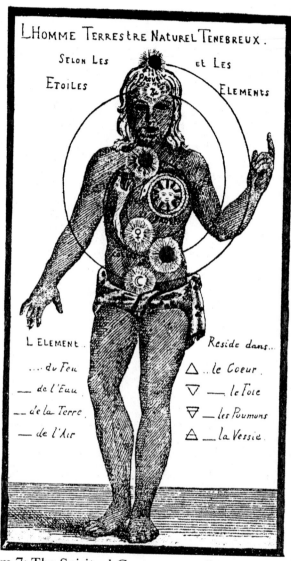

Diagram 7: The Spiritual Centers according to the German
mystic Johann Georg Gichtel.

241

THE LORD'S PRAYER AND THE SEVEN CENTERS

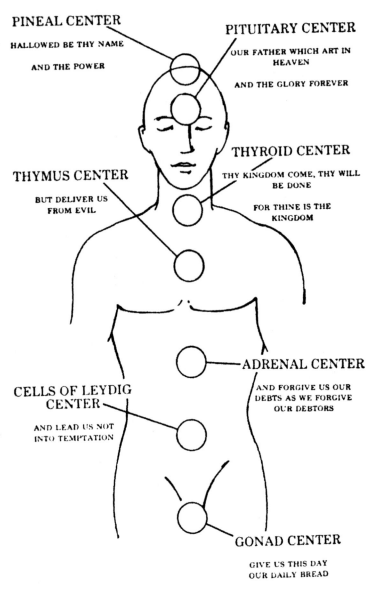

PINEAL CENTER

HALLOWED BE THY NAME

AND THE POWER

PITUITARY CENTER

OUR FATHER WHICH ART IN HEAVEN

AND THE GLORY FOREVER

THYROID CENTER

THY KINGDOM COME, THY WILL BE DONE

FOR THINE IS THE KINGDOM

THYMUS CENTER

BUT DELIVER US FROM EVIL

ADRENAL CENTER

AND FORGIVE US OUR DEBTS AS WE FORGIVE OUR DEBTORS

CELLS OF LEYDIG CENTER

AND LEAD US NOT INTO TEMPTATION

GONAD CENTER

GIVE US THIS DAY OUR DAILY BREAD

Diagram 8: The Spiritual Centers and the Lord's Prayer.

19. THE POWER WITHIN

To see what few have seen,
you must go where few have gone.

—Buddha (Siddhartha Guatama)

Usually, the most exciting experiences come as a surprise! This has been true for me in every instance. One of the most remarkable and unforgettable surprises came to me in the little town of Allegan, Michigan. Kay Tittnich was my secretary when I was teaching the Silva Method of Mind Development and Stress Control. We were invited, in the late seventies, by some friends in Allegan, to spend some time in a pyramid, that they themselves built. It was modeled after the Great Pyramid in Giza, Egypt. I believe it was about two stories high and very well constructed...there were no cracks or tiny holes anywhere. When the electric lights were turned off, we were in absolute darkness...ideal for meditation.

We spent three full days in the pyramid. We only left momentarily for basic necessities. Then, back into the pyramid! Many beautiful thoughts and images occurred to me. Without question, I felt closer to God than I ever had in my previous retreats. There were no distractions, whatsoever, after the first few hours. In continued darkness, the ego-mind was all but non-existent. By the third day, the higher mind and the spirit were in full command and the meditations were long and productive. I could mentally see things very clearly—mostly about myself: my strengths, my weaknesses, my goals, my path, my purpose in life, my relationship to the Creator, my challenges yet to come, and my reinforced views of Reality and Truth. I could honestly say it was a period of enlightenment for me.

On the third day, near the end of our glorious three-day retreat in total darkness, came the most incredible of all the surprises I was given in the pyramid. I was in a prolonged meditation, with no particular expectations, and my mind was perfectly silent. My mind was simply open and receptive, when suddenly, directly in front of me was a vivid, vibrant image of a fiery wheel of energy. I was startled at first; then, I looked at it more closely. What I saw was a four-petaled chakra. I had read about chakras, but, at that time, I could only take someone else's word for it, that they were a reality. What I saw was such a powerful force, whirling at great speed yet the *petals* (for lack of a better word) remained distinct. I could easily count them. I knew there were four! The realization that I was actually observing the base chakra, that meditators worldwide had been speaking of for centuries, was so overwhelming, I could hardly contain myself. The colors were bright red and filled the pyramid with the presence of an extraordinary energy.

Not being conscious of time, I had no idea how long I was staring at this *wonder* in front of me. I only knew that what I was witnessing would never be forgotten. It was obviously one of those once-in-a-lifetime experiences, a few of which I had become familiar. I knew in my heart that chakras are not normally visible to the human eye. At least, I had never seen one. I had to be looking at it with the inner eye, or what is also called the *third eye*. At first, I thought I was only imagining it! This was not an ordinary experience. Then I opened my eyes. It didn't matter! Whether my eyes were opened or closed, there was this magnificent fiery image whirling about. All the years that I had been meditating never resulted in anything like that. As I said before, I had no expectations meditating in the pyramid, except that it would be different...and, of course, surprises were always welcome! They seem to occur, however, when I least expect them.

I could not imagine anything more exciting happening to me in the pyramid. I was never so wrong! I was just moments away from experiencing the greatest of all surprises! As if I had not had enough spiritual excitement for one day, the brightness of the red four-petaled wheel of fire was completely overshadowed by the most powerful, dazzling force of energy I had ever seen. It was, as if I were staring at pure energy. Raw energy! Emanating straight out of the Infinite Source of all Energy. What I was looking at seemed to carry more force than many suns. It was multi-petaled! I started to count them. There were too many! This energy force was pure white in its indescribable brilliance. The thought then occurred to me: it was the thousand-petaled chakra I read about in my studies of Metaphysics. I never dreamed that I would ever *see* one in my lifetime. I cannot think of the right words to describe what I saw. I could say it was the most dazzling, radiant, resplendent and symmetrical light I had ever seen. Once again, the English language falls far short of giving my reader an adequate description. I can use all the superlatives in my vocabulary and still feel somewhat frustrated that they could not convey to you the power emanating from the highest chakra.

The energy inside of us is absolutely a Divine Energy, just as St. Peter said about the fact that we may share in the Divine Nature of God. (2 Peter 1:4) Although I could have never imagined such a powerful force in my whole life, as the kundalini power of the highest Spiritual Center, I have to say it was still second only to the Divine Light of Christ. In my book, *On My Way Home,* I spoke in detail of His extraordinary visit, in which He graced me with His Heavenly Presence, in the Church of St. Bernadette in southeast Dearborn, Michigan. There is no light or power comparable to that of the Master. And there are no words to adequately relate what I was blessed to witness. Maybe I was more overwhelmed with the breath-taking Presence of a *Person*, rather than pure *energy*.

There are a few things to explain. If you are not familiar with the Spiritual Centers in the body, allow me to share my understanding of them. The countries with the greatest history of profound meditation are all in the East. The Orientals have made meditation *a way of life.* They have studied it deeply, explored it totally and have actual experiences—giving evidence of its reality.

As I understand it, great meditators are in agreement that there are certain centers that are opened or awakened according to one's awareness or consciousness. They speak of a real power, imaged as *kundalini power.* Kundalini, in Sanskrit—a very ancient Indic language—means *serpent.* It is believed that, symbolically, there are two *serpents* coiled at the bottom of the spine, called the *ida* and the *pingala.* One is positive, the other negative. They work together! As we raise our awareness, usually in meditation (or through other insights), these coiled serpents begin to uncoil and rise up, crossing each other. They cross each other seven times. Where they first meet, is called the base center, located in the gonad area of the body. Soul forces empower the body through that area called a *chakra* or, in Sanskrit, *wheel of fire.* As the forces within rise from one center to another, the experience is accompanied by enlightenment. Surprisingly, the Spiritual Centers are associated with the Endocrine Gland System. The glands are not the source of the these spiritual energies. Rather, these powerful energies, or wheels of fire, use the Endocrine Gland System as transducers or channels, through which, spiritual power and energy is converted into *enlightenment* in the area of hormonal forces in the physical body. If you look at the chart on page 237, borrowed from the book, "The Chakras" by C.W. Leadbeater, you will see these points of contact.

This conclusion that there are seven Spiritual Centers, is drawn from their common experience of Kundalini power. When you consider all seven Centers in one glance, they take on the appearance of the symbol for the Medical Profession, called the *Caduceus,* found on page 238.

The original concept of the Caduceus goes back to the early history of the human race. It is, nevertheless, attributed to Hermes Trismegistus, the Egyptian High Priest and legendary author (and Divine Messenger), who gave the world many basic and secret Teachings. Look again at the same Diagram on page 238. The wings indicate that you would be able to fly above the material world, far above your own awareness, achieving Cosmic (or Christ) Consciousness. In this incredibly higher state of consciousness, you are able to tap into Higher Laws with abilities that are no longer hidden. Spiritual Healing is one of them. Hermes affirmed that when you awaken the highest Spiritual Center of the body, you can heal yourself spiritually and others as well.

This is a belief that has continued since ancient times. The Medical Profession, for centuries, has incorporated the idea of healing as part of its work and, therefore, use this as its medical symbol. The stress originally was on *healing* through *meditation* and *kundalini power*. For years, this idea was still in mind in the Medical Profession, but as physicians began to prescribe *medication* instead of *meditation*, the true meaning of the Caduceus was lost. Today, however, it has become fashionable among doctors to recommend meditation, in the form of guided imagery and relaxation, with or without soft music in the background—accompanied by certain medications. Doctors may or may not know the origin of the Caduceus, but it is prominently seen on their doors, on ambulances and at entrances to hospitals. The Caduceus, without question, is a modern chart of the chakras, known throughout ancient history as kundalini power.

I continued my research on meditation and discovered that experience of the Spiritual Centers is not confined to any particular type of person. As a matter of fact, every human being is capable of experiencing the same levels of consciousness, because it is a part of our Divine Heritage. Teresa of Ávila, one of my favorite Saints (and a Doctor or official Teacher of the Church), wrote a magnificent book on meditation, called *The Interior Castle*. These are her words translated from Spanish to English: "I began to think of the soul as if it were a castle made of a *single diamond,* or of very clear *crystal*, in which there are many rooms, just as, in heaven, there are many mansions." She sees seven separate mansions or levels of intimacy with God. They are not arranged according to the Endocrine Gland System, but seen rather as a crystal (in the shape of a castle) and each mansion (or level) penetrates deeper into and toward the *heart* of the crystal, where the *King of Glory* resides, according to a vision she had previously. The entire book is divided into seven parts where she describes, in detail, the advantages and challenges one encounters, as we continue the quest toward the Center of our being—the foundation of all Reality, the perfect union with the Creator. St. Teresa gives a clear description of each of the seven levels of consciousness. Here is how she describes the highest Spiritual Center or Mansion:

> Here at last the soul reaches the Spiritual Marriage (or Union.) Here dwells the King: the two lighted candles join and become one; the falling rain becomes merged in the river. There is a complete transformation, followed by ineffable and perfect peace; no higher state is conceivable, save that of the Beatific Vision (that is, seeing God face to face!) in the life to come.

There is no question about her personal experiences. She was there! She experienced it all! Like most fortunate persons, who have experienced such intimacy with God, she was reluctant to write about it. But she obeyed.

"Why do you want me to write things?" she complained to her superior. "Let learned men, who have studied, do the writing; I am a stupid creature and don't know what I am saying. There are more than enough books written on prayer already. For the love of God, let me get on with my spinning and go to choir and do my religious duties like the other Sisters. I am not meant for writing; I have neither the health nor the wits for it."

Yet, the autobiography of her life and *The Interior Castle* are classic writings in the history of Literature, and among the greatest books ever written.

In my pursuit of truth and the quest of more knowledge about meditation, I also discovered that the ancient Hebrews not only gave the world the Old Testament, but also left behind, for those who are seekers of enlightenment, the mystical teaching called the *Cabala*. The Cabala was an esoteric teaching, hidden from the general public. Recently, however, there is a renewed interest in the *Tree of Life, shown* on page 239, placing the teachings in a mystical pattern very similar to the chakras or Spiritual Centers. The above is the Sephiroth or the Tree of Life. The diagram on page 240 demonstrates the connection with the chakras along the spinal column associated with the Endocrine Gland System.

Another clairvoyant, Rudolph Steiner, an Austrian, was a contemporary of Edgar Cayce. He was a prolific author, having written about 350 volumes. One of his most famous books is *Knowledge of the Higher Worlds*, in which he explains, in detail, the Spiritual Centers from the viewpoint of Theosophy. His explanations concur with the others.

Another version occurs in the book, "Theosophia Practica," written by the well-known German mystic, Johann Georg Gichtel, a pupil of Jacob Boehme, who lived in the seventeenth century. The Diagram is found on page 241, with a notable addition. He combines the planets and the chakras, and draws a serpent through each Center, starting with the Heart Center. Gichtel's images of the Spiritual Centers display a style of Art, typical of the Far East.

By far the best documented mystic and psychic of the twentieth century is Edgar Cayce (1877-1945). His whole way of life focused on Christ and His teachings. In fact, every time he gave assistance to others, in more than 14,000 Readings, Christ was always at the center of his advice and counsel. He offered every kind service, from healing to interpreting dreams, and from good moves on the Stock Market to spiritual growth. His topics covered almost every subject one could imagine, with extraordinary accuracy. The diagram on page 242, is based on the Cayce Readings, with the Lord's Prayer related to the seven centers.

I am including this material just to show how universal these concepts are, and from totally unrelated cultures and time frames. Since we Americans have been deeply involved in industry, inventions, and high-tech developments; we have not had the history nor the intense focus on the interior life and spiritual development. But now, the time has come! There are large numbers of Americans who are ready—and from all levels of Society.

It would literally take a whole book to discuss each Spiritual Center fully. The following is a brief synopsis of each Center and its function. None of this is new, but you may or may not know what a treasure exists within you. The Endocrine Glands produce hormones for the body, when and where needed. Also, in the same area, these glands become channels for the Spiritual Centers to manifest a higher energy into the consciousness of the receiver. In this way, the Endocrine Glands act as transducers—borrowing a term from Edgar Cayce—converting energy from one form into another, just as a telephone converts electrical energy into sound, so that people may talk to each other from a distance.

Keep in mind the chart on page 242. There we see the location of each Spiritual Center. The lowest and most basic Center, called the *root chakra*, is located in the area of the gonads, within which resides the reproductive glands. It is seen as a reddish wheel of fire and, when opened, is a powerful, creative energy, which may or may not generate sexual activity, depending on whether one chooses to remain at that level or move toward the higher Spiritual Centers, achieving higher awareness.

Slightly upward along the spine, and still within the area of the reproductive system, is the second chakra, the cells of Leydig. Here is found the Center of wholeness, and the polarities of life between the male/female, the yin/yang, or the passive/active within us, resulting in *balance,* an extremely important quality in *relationships* and *spiritual growth.* Seeing only one side of an issue, adopting a small portion of truth or holding back greater enlightenment and ignoring all else, easily leads to *imbalance* or *fundamentalism.*

In the third chakra, are contained the adrenal glands, through which the consciousness is filled with power and courage at the personal, material-world level. Such courage is demonstrated in the death of martyrs, who though tortured, joyfully gave up their lives rather than their convictions. When out of balance and closed to higher subtle energies of the etheric body, the negative side dwells on resentment, anger, violence and fear. I am sure we have all experienced occasional outbursts of negative energy when harboring thoughts of anger or fear.

The fourth chakra is in the center, with three chakras below and three above. You might say, that it is the *heart* of the matter. It is actually called the Heart Center by some authorities. Human love is found here. The Spiritual Center, by name, is called the Thymus, which ordinarily produces thymazine into the system to fight off infection. It is also the Center of *human* love—but not *universal* love. When blocked, it may result in envy, jealousy or worry.

The fifth chakra focuses on the *will*. "Thy kingdom come, Thy *Will* be done on earth as it is in heaven..." We were given free will, but the higher subtle energies overwhelm our consciousness, when our will conforms to Divine Will. It is here that we prepare ourselves to be inspired by and guided by the Holy Spirit. It is found in the neck area. The Scriptures call those who stubbornly disobey the Lord as *stiff-necked* people. They actually blocked Divine Guidance. We are no exception.

The Pineal Gland or sixth chakra, is located at the top of the head. It is the seat of the soul memory and of the superconscious mind, where the intellect and intuition blend. It is not easily achieved, but its reward is magnificent! It is generally called Cosmic Consciousness or, for Christians, the Christ Consciousness. I can assure you, it does not come easily and is a quest very few pursue...but when achieved, makes life well worth living. The fifth Center is sometimes called the *cross* and the sixth, the *crown*.

We come now to the seventh Spiritual Center, in the

location of the pituitary gland. It is the highest consciousness imaginable, while still in the physical body. Here one experiences Oneness, Divine Love, Universal Love and Spiritual Healing. Those who have been there, make efforts to explain it, as did St. Teresa, but cannot convey the full impact of such an extraordinary and ecstatic experience. It is truly marvelous and indescribable. It has been known for centuries as *the third eye;* the physical eye is totally incapable of witnessing such wonders.

Summing up, let me say that the Spiritual Centers are always functioning. They are always ready to raise our awareness. They are always available to one who is open to Truth, to Divine Guidance and to the Power of God which is continually operative in the world. Because the chakras are energies of the *etheric* body, a more subtle body within us, we are not conscious of their presence ordinarily. However, when we are in church and we feel no grievance or separation from each other in our Communion...when a mother, filled with incredible strength, *instinctively* lifts a car to save her child...when you reach out to the homeless you will never see, and generously contribute to special funds for them...when true, unconditional love is expressed for another...when words like "Not my will, but Thine be done!" come out of our mouths—*these are the powerful influences of the Spiritual Centers or the Grace of God at work!* Through meditation and developing the interior life, we can be in constant contact with these powerful energies God has given to us. They can easily take us to another level! The next chapter is the key.

20. SILENCE, THE DOOR TO THE HIGHER MIND

Love cannot be far behind
a grateful heart and thankful mind...
These are the true conditions
for your Homecoming.

—A Course in Miracles

The ideal meditation brings the mind to silence. I wish to emphasize that *the silent mind* is the most powerful mind in the Universe. I am not exaggerating! To be silent to the distractions around you, to put aside your conscious mind or ego, quieting it from trying to control your whole thinking process, gives the inner mind strength. Silence does not mean a blank mind, an empty mind, a dull mind. Quite the contrary! The silent mind is fully alert, fully alive, completely ready, wide open to truth, to creativity and to Divine Action. If your ego consciousness is doing all the talking, the Divine Mind will not be heard! There is too much *noise*! In the quietness of one's being, the True Self (created in the image and likeness of God) corresponds to your level of acceptance, willingness, openness and enthusiasm. A higher level of awareness may be yours with accompanying knowledge and understanding and spiritual enlightenment.

Nevertheless, you cannot *make it happen!* If you do, you have an overactive ego, taking you on a false high to get you excited about your phenomenal growth! But, it is false and unreal. How can you tell the difference? "By their fruits you shall know them," as Jesus reminds us. If a person claims to have reached the level of the highest chakra and is filled with illumination and Divine Love, but remains a self-centered, angry individual, such a person is not really there—or even close! The ego was playing games! But if there were a radical change in the disposition and behavior of the person who claimed enlightenment and demonstrated it in daily living, with love and forgiveness, perhaps that fortunate person did reach the mountain top and truly experienced the oneness of all things.

> Infinite silence contains infinite dynamism. In this silent knowledge is a computing system that is far more precise, and far more accurate, and far more powerful than anything that is contained in the boundaries of rational thought.
>
> —Deepak Chopra

At any rate, we are not talking about a one-time experience. Meditation is an ongoing communication with our interior life and with God. One's whole day can be a prayer, moving from one fully awakened moment to another. I know it sounds like a cliché to talk about observing, for the first time, a sunset—like no other sunset—in which a person is excited for several long days...or it may be the observance of a flower, or a smile on a child's face. These, I know, are typical examples of raising one's awareness, but I am referring to that particular moment—like no other moment ever before—in which such inexpressible beauty reminds us of the Beauty and Grandeur of God. It may be a once-in-a-life-time gift from above. The flowers or objects of beauty don't change..we do! It is that rare occasion when the observer and the observed become one! With no separation! In fact, in that precious moment, that holy instant, to use an expression from ACIM, you sensed yourself being one with all things, not just the flower or the sunset. Believe me, this does not happen often.

I recall in 1971, on one of the early days of Spring, I was returning to St. Bernadette Parish from the bank. Something urged me to go back another way, a longer way. As I was driving through Hines Park with beautiful trees everywhere, I suddenly stopped and parked the car. I would not be able to explain why I parked in that particular spot, if someone asked me. I got out of my car and walked toward a single tree. I did something there that was most peculiar! I hugged a tree! I *loved* that tree! It was fully alive and so was I. We were one! I then stood on a rock; it felt like it was an extension of me. Only when I got there, did I notice a stream with running water. I moved over to the water and splashed myself in the face a few times. I was touching another part of me. I did not see the outward forms around me. I saw and felt their *essence*. It was the same as mine. There no longer was a world out there! I was the world and the world was I...all extensions of the great Power of God. And yes! I once again felt that inexpressible closeness to God. I began to see Nature from another viewpoint. Having such an unforgettable experience of *oneness* through Nature, also happened on other rare occasions. As I said, these peak moments of enlightenment, as with meditation in a sitting position, do not happen often. But if you are consistently open, this form of meditation brings illumination more and more frequently.

Most often, what happens, occurs as a total surprise. I used to teach the Silva Method when I was at Most Holy Trinity Church. Every few months I would have a guest speaker come in and address my graduates with a lecture—pertinent to some topic in the Mind Development Course, e.g. dreams, pain or the body/mind connection, etc. Frankly, I do not remember the topic of that particular lecture, but I do remember something that happened, which I shall never forget. There were about one hundred and twenty-five persons in the lecture room (actually the school cafeteria.) I stood in the back, near the entrance. I was listening to the lecture, when suddenly, I was no longer listening to what was being said. My conscious mind was totally silent. I looked at the people sitting there. They no longer appeared separate, each one in their own space! They were spirits listening. They all appeared alike with a bright, whitish aura and each one blended into the ones around them. There were no male or female listeners. They were not separate! Well, it's hard to explain what I saw: they were indeed *individuals,* but, at the same time, they were all *one* also. I kept staring and got very excited. I had heard about such things being possible, but I never thought I would see this rare occurrence with my own eyes. I looked at my own hands and legs—it was the same essence, with no distinction between them and myself. In the next moment, there was an even greater surprise! I felt oneness with *everything,* even the blackboard in the room and the building itself. Yes, everything! I said to myself once again: *So that's what my Divine Guide meant when He said so many times: "All is one!"* I was grateful to the Lord for giving me this experience.

This unexpected experience that belongs to the highest awareness within us; this grandest view imaginable, lasted about five minutes. It seemed like it was forever! And I wished it was! Like I said, these experiences don't happen often, but they *do* happen and are more likely to be seen by a mind that is pure and simple—"Unless you become as a little child..."—or to a mind that has learned through meditation to expect the unexpected. I try to remain open and ready to receive at all times. There is only one problem: neither you nor I can make an authentic spiritual experience take place. It isn't within our domain of power.

People have told me that they reach a very high level of spiritual excitement when they see "Touched by an Angel" on television. I have watched that program when I am able to, and yes, it can bring a person to silence, when you see two people joined together, where there was hatred, division or separation before. Their reunion, their reconciliation, their oneness at the end of the story can leave the viewer somewhat teary-eyed. But more than that, certain feelings emerge that were repressed, raising one's awareness, even if it is only for a precious moment. According to ACIM, where there was enmity between two persons and they are joined as one, the place where they stand is holy ground.

One way to have *thoughts of oneness* is through movies, stories, and in general, the lives and experiences of others. This does not take the place of meditating or observing the world around you. There is much to learn from television, but it is not your world. I hope it is not! Granted, God can open your eyes through any medium: a television set, the ocean, a child, soft rain and so forth. And it's wonderful! However, don't give up the effort of uniting yourself to God through prayer and meditation. Daily, if possible!

I have made a deep study of meditation. I have read many

authors. The book that appeals most to me, is "The New Seeds of Contemplation" by Thomas Merton, a Trappist monk, who died in the early sixties. In another part of this book I speak about his visitation to me at about 4:00 a.m. when he encouraged me to read his books. This book I keep re-reading from time to time. It sums up what I needed to know about *infused contemplation* or *mysticism*. I believe he truly experienced the above, because he speaks with clarity and authenticity about what contemplation is, and what it is not! Contemplation, in the sense that it is explained in his book, refers to the highest, most profound experience of enlightenment or oneness with God, while still on the earth plane.

In theological terms, there is the *purgative, illuminative* and *unitive way* of relating to God. I believe Merton's view of *contemplation* is the unitive way which, by far, is the highest awareness of the three.

First, what contemplation is not:

It is not philosophical; it is not a static awareness of spiritual things that are never changing. It is not a contemplation of abstract ideas. Contemplation cannot be objectively or scientifically analyzed; it cannot be put into words exactly or reasoned out. There is no definition for the contemplative experience because, in an attempt to define it, one has to proceed psychologically, and there does not exist an adequate psychology of contemplation.

To describe one's reactions and feelings, is to place contemplation where it is not to be found: in the superficial consciousness where it can be observed by reflection. The conscious mind is a part of that external self which *dies* and is cast aside, like a soiled garment, in the genuine awakening of the contemplative. Contemplation is not and cannot be a function of the external self. When we use the superficial "I", we are not referring to our real Self. For example, to say "I need a drink!" or "I feel sick!", we are speaking as the *ego,* which can be studied or analyzed.

The "I" that works in the world, thinks about itself, observes its own reaction and talks about itself, is not the True Self that was created in the image and likeness of God. The ego is, at best, merely the vesture, the mask, the disguise of that mysterious and unknown Divine Image within us, whom most of us never discover, until our life here is ended. Our external self or ego is not eternal nor spiritual—far from it! This ego-self is doomed to disappear as completely as smoke from a chimney.

Contemplation is not just an affair of a passive and quiet temperament, nor is it a tendency to inactivity or psychic peace. One who experiences contemplation is not merely a person who likes to sit and think, still less a person who sits around with a vacant stare. Having a thoughtful and reflective disposition is certainly beneficial in this world of confusion and may very well dispose a person for contemplation. But that is not it!

Contemplation is not prayerfulness or a tendency to find peace and satisfaction in Liturgical Rites. These, too, are a great good, and they are almost necessary preparations for the contemplative experience. But they can never, of themselves, constitute the experience. A person with a quiet temperament may become a contemplative, but temperament has nothing to do with contemplation and can even be an obstacle to the inner struggle and crisis, through which one comes to a deeper spiritual awakening. It is possible, according to Merton, for an active and passionate person to awaken to contemplation, but not likely. Such people, being given to imagination, passion and active conquest, exhaust themselves in trying to attain contemplation, as if it were some kind of object, like a treasure, or a political office, or a professorship or becoming a president of a company.

Contemplation can never be an object of calculated ambition or something we plan to obtain with our practical knowledge and techniques. It is not *we,* who choose to awaken ourselves, but *God* Who chooses to awaken us. Contemplation is not trance or ecstasy, nor the hearing of unutterable words nor the imagination of lights. It is not the emotional fire and aptness that come with religious exultation. It is not enthusiasm, or the sense of being "seized" by an elemental force and swept into liberation by mystical frenzy. All of these things may seem to be a contemplative awakening since one's ordinary awareness and control are suspended and may be accompanied by a religious experience. But they are not the work of the *higher self, guided by the Holy Spirit.*

Nor is contemplation the gift of prophecy or tongues, nor does it imply the psychic ability to read the secrets of people's lives. Sometimes true contemplation is accompanied by them, but they are not essential to it.

> For instance, the experience of being seized and taken out of oneself by collective enthusiasm...in the self-righteous upsurge of party loyalty or ecstatic enthusiasm generated by a powerful politician or rock concert. These are real *highs* but not in the same category as contemplation. Nor is an escape from conflict, from anguish or from doubt!
>
> —Merton

Hence, it is clear that genuine contemplation is incompatible with complacency and with smug acceptance of prejudicial opinion. It is not mere passive approval of the "Status quo" as some would like to believe—since this would reduce it to the level of *spiritual anesthesia*! And it is not a pain-killer. Lastly, contemplation is not something we can attain alone, by our own intellectual effort, by perfecting our natural powers, nor by self-hypnosis. All of the above is what contemplation is *not*!

If you will walk with me in patience, we will review what Infused Contemplation *is*. You may be wondering: "What's left?"

The experience of true contemplation occurs like a holocaust, in the steady burning to ashes of old worn-out words, clichés, slogans and rationalizations! Even some apparently *holy* concepts are consumed with all the rest. It is a terrible breaking and burning of idols and a purification of the sanctuary, so that no graven things may occupy the place that God has commanded to be left empty: the center of our being, the sacred altar within us, wherein dwells the Holy Spirit.

Contemplation is the expression of a person's intellectual and spiritual life. It is that life itself, fully awake, fully active, and fully aware that it is alive. It is a spiritual wonder and the spontaneous awe at the sacredness of life. It is gratitude for life and for awareness. Contemplation is a vivid realization that all life in us proceeds from an invisible, transcendent and infinitely abundant Source. In fact, contemplation *knows* the Source, with a certainty that goes beyond reason and beyond simple faith. Actually reason and faith reach out by their very nature to contemplation, for without it, they would be incomplete. Yet we can say that contemplation is not vision because it sees, without seeing, and knows, without knowing. Knowledge and faith, nurtured by contemplation, are so profound that they are too deep to be grasped in images, in words or even in clear concepts. In contemplation, one knows beyond all knowing.

Although poetry, music and art have something in common with it, contemplative experience is beyond aesthetic intuition, beyond art, beyond poetry, beyond philosophy, beyond speculative theology. In a sense, it fulfills them all, and then passes by them like the speed of light, as if they didn't exist!

Contemplation is always beyond our own knowledge, beyond our understanding, beyond our own belief systems, beyond explanation, beyond dialogue and, yes, beyond our own self. You might say that to enter into the realm of contemplation, one must, in a certain sense, *die—yes! Dying to oneself* prepares us for entrance into another dimension, a higher consciousness, a higher life. It is death, for the sake of life, which leaves behind all that we can know or treasure as life, as thought, as experience, as joy, as being.

St. Thomas Aquinas wrote the most eloquent volumes of theology and philosophy. They are considered a masterpiece and have been the basis of the theology and philosophy in the West for the last seven hundred years. Yet, near the end of his life, he considered his magnificent works as mere straw to be burned—compared to the reality of his mystical experience with God. In his estimation, what he wrote sadly paled in the Presence of Divine Truth.

Again, contemplation is compatible with all of the above and is their highest fulfillment! But at a certain point, all other experiences are momentarily lost—they die that we may be born anew! Contemplation reaches out to the transcendent and inexpressible God, Who is Absolute Reality and the Source of all that is Real. Unfortunately, most of what we know, on our own, is *illusion*. Contemplation is a response to a *call* by One Who speaks to the depths of our own being. In response, the contemplative echos the Creator with a deep, cosmic resonance in the innermost center of his or her being. God actually answers Himself in us and this answer is Divine Life, Divine Creativity, making all things new! We ourselves become His echo and His answer! It is as if in creating us, God asked a question, and in awakening us to contemplation, He answered the question. And all is summed up in one awareness—not a proposition, but an experience: "I am."

This religious and transcendent contemplation is truly a *gift*. St. Paul, once again, offers this insight, "The Spirit Himself gives testimony to our own spirit that we are sons (and daughters) of God."

Contemplation is more than a consideration of abstract truths about God, even more than effective meditation on the things we believe. It is the awakening, the enlightenment and the amazing intuitive grasp by which love gains certitude of God's creative and dynamic intervention in our daily life.

Contemplation does not simply *discover* or *find* a clear idea of God, or confine Him within our limits of that idea, and hold Him there like a prisoner. It is quite the contrary! The person, in pure contemplation, is literally carried away by God into His own Realm, His own Mystery and His own Freedom. Obviously, if you have ever experienced contemplation, it would be absolutely unforgettable!

Most people meditating, will be located somewhere between the simplest forms of meditation and the ultimate experience of contemplation. If there is a sincere effort, *all levels of meditation are beneficial, wholesome and acceptable.* It is not necessary that everyone be able to achieve the dimension of contemplation as explained above. And that is all right. I am simply offering the highest forms of meditation that I am personally aware of, and therefore, am able to share these with you. There may be more profound levels of meditation that are beyond my knowledge, but I would prefer not to share experiences that are spiritually beyond my present capacity. *Believe me, it is not arrogance!* It is just the opposite. I still have not figured out why God has favored me with such experiences. But I feel impelled to share them with those who are ready for the next step or to dialogue with those who have already been there. More than anything, I am completely humbled by these experiences...and my life has never been the same.

I encourage you to continue seeking an intimate communication with God. At some point in your quest, your Infinitely Loving Parent will take you well beyond the limitations of your conscious mind. The greatest powers given to a human being are the invisible, creative forces hidden within us. They await your pursuit—to be awakened by the Divine Power Who put them there.

Whenever you feel or believe that you are powerless, read the words of Psalm 8:3-6, paraphrased to make them inclusive. It should lift your spirits:

Lord, when I look at the sky, which you have made,
at the moon and the stars,
which you set in their places—
what are we, that you think of us;
mere men and women, that you care for us?
Yet, you made us inferior only to yourself,
you crowned us with glory and honor.
You appointed us rulers over
everything you made;
you placed us over all creation.

CONCLUSION

Excuse me for ending with a poem, but I could not say what I wanted to, in ordinary prose. The following is not just fantasy. It is based on the principles of ACIM as well as my own reflections on *our journey without distance to a place (God's Presence) we have never left.*

I believe we have missed a very important aspect in our desire to go to heaven and live happily ever after with God in the Kingdom.

Have you given much thought to this quote from Sacred Scripture? In Luke 17:21-22, it reads:

> The Kingdom of God does not come in such a way as to be seen. No one will say, "Look, here it is!" or, "There it is!", because *the Kingdom of God is within you.*

If God's Kingdom is within us or among us, how do we get away from it? We can only imagine or believe in our own mind that we are separate from God, when, in reality, we are not!

We were all created in God's image outside of time and space. We were an idea in the Mind of God, eons before we were actually born into this physical world. God lives in a

World or Kingdom of Spirit. The Kingdom of God has always existed and will exist forever and we are part of that Creation. Each of us has a level of fulfillment waiting for us in the next life. We are not talking about a *place or location* somewhere out there! We are talking about a *State of Consciousness.*

This is what Pope John Paul II said in his general Wednesday audience, on July 21, 1999:

Heaven is not an abstraction nor a physical place amid the clouds, but a living and personal relationship with the Holy Trinity. *A week later he followed up with:* More than a physical place, hell is the state of those who freely and definitively separate themselves from God, the source of all life and joy. Hell is the pain, frustration and emptiness of life without God...Eternal damnation is not God's work, but our own doing.

He concluded that a foretaste of Heaven can be experienced partially on earth. I believe that Meditation, Holy Eucharist, Spiritual Healing, awakening the higher Spiritual Centers, acts of unconditional Love, forgiveness and other inspiring activities *do* make it possible to catch a glimpse of our eternal Home, the Kingdom of God! Though we may not realize it consciously, we *are* already there! That is why we call it

Home. As we mature spiritually, we are in the process of remembering who we are. I use the word *remembering* deliberately. If we were once created in God's image, that fact can never change! We are God's Creations forever! What God wills, will always be. God is All-Powerful and Infinite, without equal. There is no other power in the Universe to change God's Will.

We can, however, with our free will, choose to delude or deceive ourselves with incorrect concepts. Even though the thought would be an illusion, a false belief in separation or a distorted view of ourselves and reality, we *still remain* God's sons and daughters in the Eternal Kingdom, regardless of our illusion to the contrary.

> *He never wasted a leaf or a tree.*
> *Do you think He would squander souls?*
> —Rudyard Kipling

The strangest part of this story is that we have never left God, nor our blissful state of consciousness in the Kingdom. *We thought we did...and still do!* I repeat this most tragic misunderstanding: We set ourselves on a journey without distance to a place we have never left. Reflecting on this uncanny situation, I wrote the following:

IN MY FATHER'S HOUSE

Before time ever began,
I was an idea in the Mind of God.
I was always there,
and there I will always be.

One day, many eons past,
a thought occurred to me:
My Father's House is absolutely Perfect...
maybe I can do what he did, and even better!

So I slipped outside my Home,
as did many of my siblings.
We had fun exploring, making something new.
But the Spirit said: "You really did not move out."

Thinking we did, we forgot to laugh at ourselves.
Soon, we didn't like what we did,
and the fun turned sour. We had to hide.
We knew one place where God would not find us.

We quickly scattered to a world of illusion.
It was unreal. So, He would not be there!
But the Spirit reminded us once again:
"You never left your Home! Wake up!"

Ah! But no! We covered ourselves in shame,
believing there is only one way Home—the long way!
Soon, the Spirit's Voice became very soft, then silent,
and we followed a course that took us far from Home.

Thank God, we are living in the Age of Salvation!
God's Love is constant, and so is His Presence.
The Kingdom of Heaven is within us! (Thank you, Jesus!)
Open your eyes and enjoy the Truth.

We belong to God and we always will.
There is no death, there is no time...
God is all! And where God is—
We shall always be!

—Rev. Jay Samonie

BIBLIOGRAPHY

Anderson, U. S., 1964. *Three Magic Words*. No. Hollywood, California: Wilshire Book Company.

Bristol, Claude M. 1972. *The Magic of Believing*. New York: Picket Books.

Brown, Barbara B. 1974. *New Mind, New Body*. New York: Harper & Row.

Davis, Roy Eugene. 1968. *The Way of the Initiate*. Lakemont, Georgia: CSA Press.

Dechanet, J.M. 1971. *Yoga in Ten Lessons*. New York: Cornerstone Library.

De Chardin, Teilhard. 1965. *Hymn of the Universe*. New York: Harper & Row.

Fenwick, Peter. 1995. An investigation of over 300 near-death experiences. *The Truth in the Light*. New York: Berkley Books

Germain, Walter M. 1956. *The Magic Power of your Mind*. No. Hollywood, California: Wilshire Book Company.

Goldsmith, Joel S. 1963. *The Contemplative Life*. Secaucus, New Jersey: The Citadel Press.

Jampolsky, Gerald G. 1970. *Love is Letting Go of Fear*. New York: Bantam Books.

Holmes, Ernest, and Willis Kinnear. 1982. *The Magic of the Mind*. Los Angeles: Science of Mind Publications.

Kelsey, Morton T. 1976. A guide to Christian meditation. *The Other Side of Silence.* New Jersey, Paulist Press.

Leadbeater, C. W. 1927. *The Chakras.* Wheaton, Illinois: Quest Books.

LeShan, Lawrence. 1974. *How to Meditate.* New York: Bantam Books.

Maltz, Maxwell. 1960. Self-image and the subconscious mind. *Psycho-Cybernetics.* New Jersey: Prentice-Hall, Inc.

Merton, Thomas. 1961. *New Seeds of Contemplation.* New York: New Directions Publishing Corporation.

Murphy, Joseph. 1963. *The Power of Your Subconscious Mind.* New Jersey: Prentice-Hall, Inc.

O'Murchu, Diarmuid. 1997. *Quantum Theology.* New York: The Crossroad Publishing Company.

Peale, Norman Vincent. 1952. *The Power of Positive Thinking.* New York: Fawcett Crest.

Powell, A. E. 1925. *The Etheric Double.* Wheaton, Illinois. Quest Books.

Puryear, Herbert B. And Mark A. Thurston. 1975. *Meditation and the Mind of Man.* Virginia Beach: A.R.E. Press.

Rheeders, Kate. 1996. *Qabalah, A Beginner's Guide.* London, England: Headway-Hodder & Stoughton.

Ring, Kenneth and Evelyn Elsaesser Valarino. 1998. What we can learn from the near-death experience. *Lessons from the Light.* New York: Plenum Press.

Ritchie, George G. 1978. A well-documented near-death experience by a physician. *Return from Tomorrow.* Grand Rapids, Michigan: Fleming H. Revell.

Russell, Edward. 1971. *Design for Destiny.* London, England: Neville Spearman.

Russell, Marjorie. 1978. *A Handbook of Christian Meditation.* Old Greenwich, Connecticut.: Devin-Adair.

Samonie, Jay. 1998. *On My Way Home.* Kearney, Nebraska: Morris Publishing.

Teresa of Ávila. 1579, Translation, 1961. A guide to meditation. *Interior Castle.* New York: Doubleday.

Van Auken, John. 1992. *Spiritual Breakthrough.* Virginia Beach: A.R.E. Press.

Valarino, Evelyn Elsaesser. 1997. Exploring the phenomenon of the near-death experience. *On the Other Side of Life.* New York: Plenum Press.

Williams, John K. 1964. *The Wisdom of Your Subconscious Mind.* New Jersey: Prentice-Hall, Inc.

To order additional copies of "Reflections on My Way Home", complete the information below.

Mail to: (please print)

Name_____

Address_____

City, State, Zip_____

Day phone (_____)_____

___copies of "Reflections on My Way Home" @ $14.95

Michigan tax @ .90 per book _____

Shipping and handling @ $2.00

per book (or every 2 books) _____

Total amount enclosed $_____

Make checks payable to Rev. Jay Samonie

Send to:

Rev. Jay J. Samonie

34664 Spring Valley Dr.

Westland, MI 48185-9457